W. Flexney Holborn

Dialogues of Lucian From the Greek

Vol. I

W. Flexney Holborn

Dialogues of Lucian From the Greek
Vol. I

ISBN/EAN: 9783741191879

Manufactured in Europe, USA, Canada, Australia, Japa

Cover: Foto ©Andreas Hilbeck / pixelio.de

Manufactured and distributed by brebook publishing software (www.brebook.com)

W. Flexney Holborn

Dialogues of Lucian From the Greek

Vol. I

Dialogues of Lucian

From the Greek

Second Edition

London, Printed in the Year 1774

for W. Fleaxney Holborn

TO
THE MEMORY
OF
GEORGE LORD LYTTELTON,
AND TO
THE CANDOUR OF THE PUBLICK,
THIS SECOND EDITION OF
THE FIRST VOLUME OF
AN ATTEMPT TO TRANSLATE LUCIAN,
IS DEDICATED
WITH DEFERENCE AND GRATITUDE.

> That fire of Genius can be brought
> To kindle only where it ought,
> With virtue nobly can conform,
> Nor, wild with power, impale a worm;
> When will this futile age afford
> A proof like thee, lamented Lord?

PREFACE.

FROM what little I have been able to conjecture of the spirit of those who sit in judgment on authors, I am induced to believe, that humble supplications avail but little. The ingenuous require no soothing, and nothing could soften the hard heart of supercilious severity. My few friends, who will read this translation, are not likely to be biassed by any unfair representation of it; and, if it is decried with justice, I shall complain of nothing so much as my own folly. I only beg of the wanton talkers, who have more wit than they know what to do with, that they will be graciously pleased to recollect the remonstrance of Æsop's frogs. Before they bestow those angry appellations on dulness, which are only due to vice, it might not be altogether amiss, if they were to consider their duty towards their neighbour. The most inveterate scribbler, who means no harm,

harm, is not the worst character in a community. And mediocrity, one would think, need not appear so abominable in the eyes of stupidity.

But it is difficult for a man to be convinced to his satisfaction of his own scanty intellect, and various are the methods made use of to shift the imputation to another. When, with an air of false modesty, he affects to think himself nothing at all, how little does he wish to be believed! when scorn has found some other object, glad to be safe himself, with hostile joy he eyes the victim—

> *quæ sibi quisque timebat,*
> *Unius in miseri exitium conversa tulere.*

Claiming the privilege of being tried by my peers, I beg leave to except against the following persons as incompetent: those who read intending to be angry, those who read expecting to be pleased, and those who cannot read at all. To exhibit a translation, that shall in any degree resemble an original, is not so very easy as several persons, who have never tried, may imagine. In order to make a comparison, it will be very useful to understand something of each language. I will put the case, O gentle censor, to thy conscience. If, when thou openest thine eyes upon Lucian, thy prevailing idea be that of crabbed Greek, be assured of thy fallibility in this matter. Get more strength, and thou wilt learn forgiveness.

To mention one's own transgression affords but little delight. But the reader would find out mine without any assistance, and I will be beforehand with him. Having been instructed in the laws of translation, it would be in vain to deny the presumption of wilful infringement. To preserve the sense and spirit and turn and temper and wit and genius of an ancient author, a translator should possess them all himself. He may speak a different language, and live in a different age; but little more abatement will be made him. This is the law. But where are such translators to be found? After Dryden and a few others, what man of genius will put on painful shackles, and tamely sit down to translate? who that can be original will be contented with imitation; and especially when imitation is so very imperfect?

For after all that can be done, whoever desires to be well acquainted with an ancient author, must take the trouble of learning his language [b]. He will then allow of originals and translations, as of family quarrels, that there may be faults on both sides.

There is a translation of Lucian, which is commonly called Dryden's, perhaps from a sense of justice to some bookseller, who had paid a sum of money, that it might be called so. "Unhappy Dryden!"

The translation by Mr. Francis Hickes appears, by the language, to have been made about the beginning of the last century. At least it was before that of Jasper Mayne, done in 1638, and published in 1664. Their translations taken together extend to only a small part of Lucian. In his dedication to the Marquis of Newcastle, Dr. Mayne complains bitterly of persons who " do defile the English

---

[b] If, after being charmed with the beauties of Pope's Homer, a person should make himself master of the original, how would he be surprised,

"To see
How all things differ, where they all agree!"

tongue

tongue with *republick* words." The diction, which then prevailed, might very well provoke the good Doctor to differ from Longinus and others, in his opinion concerning the rise of eloquence.

Spence, according to Lord Dorset, " was so cunning a translator, that a man must read the original to understand the version." Mr. Spence's wit has but little of the Attick elegance of Lucian, but a great deal of the facetious [*c*] Mr. Punch.

These are all the English translations of Lucian, that I have seen. That of D'Ablancourt into French has been the most read. Though Lucian was no niggard of his speech, Monsieur D'Ablancourt found him unlike a Frenchman, and new-modelled him accordingly. Spence's

[*c*] He wanted to be thought *comical*, which was the character Eunapius had given his author. Αστειος ἡ τα Εμφορωμεν αυτε σπεδαιις ις το γελασθηναι. Phædrus, who was a translator very different from Mr. Spence, intended the same effect. " Duplex libelli dos est, quod risum movet." In former days the risible muscles must have been moved by a very light touch. A sober Englishman would stare to see a reader laugh at Æsop's fables, and think him almost as strange a fellow as Æsop himself.

English is nothing more than an aukward copy of D'Ablancourt's French.

The pieces in this volume do not follow one another in the same order as in the original. Had I begun translating with an intention of going through the whole of Lucian's works, I might probably have observed the common order; though with no other reason than the usage of Editors. But no man will wish to translate the [d] whole of Lucian, who thinks the world already bad enough, and, though he cannot make it better, does not desire to make it worse.

The Editors of other trifles may have been misled by learned advisers. Unfortunately for me, my errors are all my own. I make no part of a little knot of little authors, who, joining their stock together, launch into the deep on a broader bottom. My consolation is that of the single adventurer, whose good or bad success affects only himself. No " frowning judge" can bring my friends to shame. And

[d] Duplex omnino est jocandi genus. Cicero de Off. lib. i. To humble the pride of genius, fine sense and folly have been seen together in every age.

if, in the wonderful variety of every day's incidents, some scattered particle of praise should be blown in my way, I will gather it up as clean as I can, and greedily devour it, without asking [e] questions.

I hope no enquiry will be made into the motives of this undertaking, of which I confess myself unable to give any satisfactory account. The advertiser of a new Magazine had the kindness to offer " a work much wanted." The world may be in need of a new magazine; but I have some reason to think, that it is not greatly distressed for want of my translation. Persons in distress are apt now and then to complain, and I have been peaceably suffered entirely to neglect it for almost the nine years assigned to

" The last and greatest art, the art to blot."

From this patient forbearance of the publick I conclude, that very few will be displeased

[e] While I was writing this sentence, an indignant volume of *Reviews* descended hastily from an upper shelf, and narrowly missed my head. ☞ The danger is now past. Not so the joyful remembrance of so unpromising an omen!

with

with me for intending never more to trouble them with *Proposals for printing a book* [*f*]. I return thanks to the voluntary subscribers. It was not my fault, that a gentleman's name was printed without his consent, nor that he does not "*understand* such odd stuff."

No reckless intruder appears in the Title-page. The inclemency of reading has been known to spend itself there; and a name, unsheltered with academical honours, stands less exposed at the end of a Preface.

JOHN CARR.

[*f*] When this Preface appeared before, I had no intention of continuing the translation in any mode whatever, nor any thoughts of a new Edition. But, after some experience of the publick favour, I found myself very little disposed to question its propriety; and my publisher, who believes strongly in the mutability of men's dispositions, gave me such powerful reasons for a speedy republication, that I changed my mind.

"He cannot tell what criticks thought it,
He only knows, that people bought it."

SOME ACCOUNT

OF THE

LIFE OF LUCIAN.

LUCIAN was born at Samosata, a city of Syria, near the Euphrates. The time of his birth is uncertain; but it appears, from the persons, authors, and events, which he mentions, that he flourished under the Antonines and Commodus. If his dialogues had come down to us in the order of time in which they were written, it would have been easier to fix, or at least to guess at, the year in which he was born. His parents are said to have been originally of Patræ, in Achaia; though, in the dream which he relates, there are no traces of family pride. His father, he says, not know-

ing

ing how to support him at home, put him apprentice to a stone-cutter. This stone-cutter was his uncle, who, having observed in the boy a talent, as he thought, for his trade, was at first greatly pleased with his disciple. But, an unlucky accident occasioning a quarrel between them, Lucian, in the pride and naughtiness of his heart, ran home to his mother to complain. He does not say, that she pointed out to him the path he was by nature fitted to pursue, but that two other females scolded him into it. He left his country, and improved himself so much by travelling, that no man nowadays can distinguish him from a native Athenian. He taught rhetorick in Gaul and other places. In Antioch he was a pleader at the bar. In this profession he took a dislike to noise and lying, and sate down to write dialogues on the folly of mankind. He was about forty years of age when he began to imagine himself wiser than the philosophers of his time, with whose respective lives and opinions he was well enough acquainted to have abundant matter for ridicule. He makes continual allusions

to

to Homer, perhaps thinking himself, like Persius, a wiser man than the writer of an Iliad.

"*Hoc ridere meum, tam nil, nullâ tibi vendo Iliade.*"

In his old age he was appointed to some place of consequence under the Emperor in Ægypt, though it is not easy to determine exactly what. He married when somewhat advanced in age, and had a son, who was a favourite with Julian. A letter of that Emperor to him is still extant. The same talents, that recommended the father to Aurelius, appear to have been possessed in some degree by the son. It is most probable that Lucian died about the age of ninety towards the end of the second century; and it is more likely that he died of the gout than that he was devoured by dogs enraged to find an apostate. The story of his embracing and afterwards renouncing the Christian religion, with that [b] dreadful consequence, seems to have been the invention of some bigot absurd enough to dream of an alliance between truth and falshood.

[g] Zuingerus has disposed of Lucian's body and soul to his heart's content. "*Quare et rabici illius pœnas sufficientes in præsenti vita dedit, et in futurum hæres eternal ignis una cum Satana erit.*"

The style of Lucian being more pure than that of his contemporaries, two or three of the most celebrated fathers are reported to have improved themselves in composition by studying his works, and to have turned the artillery of his wit against his own party. Those who are conversant with the fathers may possibly know where this wit is written,

[xv]

Λυκιανυ εις την ἑαυτυ βιβλον.

Λυκιανος ταδ' εγραψα, [b] παλαια τε μωρα τε ειδως,
Μωρα γαρ ανθρωποις και τα δοκευντα σοφα.
Ουδεν εν ανθρωποισι διακριδον εςι νοημα;
Αλλ' ὁ συ θαυμαζεις, τοδ' ἑτεροισι γελως.

LUCIAN on his Book.

I Lucian from the life this picture drew
Of errors old, of follies not a few,
Difcordant judgments find no general rule,
Maid to admire, and rafh to ridicule.

[b] Παλαια τε πολλα τε ιδυς. Hom. Od. vii. ver. 157.

THE

THE

DREAM:

OR,

LUCIAN's Account of HIMSELF.

B

THE DREAM[a].

I WAS now a great boy, and had left off going to school, when my father began to confult with our friends what he fhould make of me. Moft of them were of opinion, that a learned profeffion required a plentiful fortune; time, pains, and expence, being equally neceffary: whereas our circumftances were fuch as ftood much in need of fpeedy amendment. "But, if I were to learn a trade, I might not

---

[a] This Dream is an imitation of THE CHOICE OF HERCULES, a well-known ftory in Xenophon's Memorabilia of Socrates. The Englifh reader may fee it in the Tatler N° 97, and in Spence's Polymetis. Xenophon had it from Prodicus, who, he fays, told it in a better manner. Lucian might have faid the fame of Xenophon.

only be able to live of myself, without encumbering my father, now that I was grown up; but, in a little time, might fill him with joy, to see me bring home the fruits of my labours." The next question to be resolved, was, what was the best trade, the easiest to be acquired, the most genteel, the least expensive in setting up, and affording the fairest prospect of gain. While one recommended one thing, and another another, according to his own experience or caprice, my father, casting his eyes on my uncle, who was an excellent Statuary, declared, that no other trade but his ought to be named in his presence. " Take him, said he, (pointing to me) and make him perfect in your business: you know him to be a lad of parts, who will do you credit." He presumed this from some toys he had seen of my making. For I had been used, when out of my schoolmaster's sight, to get wax, and scrape it into twenty odd figures, such as oxen, horses, or men; which my father (poor man!) thought very fine, but for which my master used to beat me. Upon the strength of this I was encouraged to go on, as there could be no doubt of my soon becoming a master of my trade, after these voluntary specimens of dexterity. I was therefore without loss of time given up to my uncle, without betraying or feeling much dissatisfaction; for I could not but think it convenient enough to have the opportunity, whenever I would, of pleasing myself, or obliging my friend, with a god or a hero of my own making. So I was entered in the usual manner. My uncle gave me a chisel, and bade me use it gently, repeating the proverb, *A good beginning makes a good end.* But, for want of knowing better, I hit too hard, and broke the marble. My uncle, enraged, snatching up a whip, belaboured me in such a manner as made me shed many tears, and gave me no great stomach to the trade. Blubbering most sadly I ran home with my story, shewing the weals, and recounting my uncle's cruelty; saying, I was sure it was envy, and nothing else, that made him use me so. My mother kindly heard me, and heartily abused her tyrant of a brother. All that night I spent in sobbing and thinking.—What I have hitherto said seems the trifling of a child; but what

is to come, Gentlemen, will require your patient attention. As Homer says, "A divine vision of the ambrosial night appeared in a dream," so plain that reality itself could not be more so: for even to this moment I think I hear and see all that I did then. Two women laid hold of me, and pulled me different ways, each to herself, with such violence that I feared they would have torn me in pieces between them. Now one prevailed, and then the other. Then they scolded most bitterly; the one declaring she wanted only her own, and the other protesting that her antagonist should lose her labour. The one was a masculine creature, made for hard work, with hair neglected, hands callous, gown tucked up, all over dust; in short, just like my uncle, when he polished his marble. The other had a beautiful face, a graceful person, an elegant dress. After much contention they referred the matter to me. And first that hard-favoured robust animal began: "I, my dear boy, am "Statuary, to whose acquaintance you were "yesterday to be introduced. I am your friend "and relation. Your grandfather (naming my
"mother's

"mother's father) was a stone-cutter, as well
"as your two uncles, who became both very
"famous by means of me. If then you can
"resolve with yourself to renounce the trifles
"which she would tempt you with (pointing
"to the other), and come and dwell with me,
"in the first place, you shall live like a man,
"you shall be hale and strong, you shall escape
"all envy; you shall have no occasion to seek
"a foreign land, leaving your relations and
"country, for the praise of an empty speech.
"Disdain not the mean appearance of my per-
"son and apparel. It was from such a be-
"ginning that Phidias, the carver of Jove, laid
"the foundation of his fame. You have heard
"too of Polycletus, who made a Juno; of
"the praises of Myron and Praxiteles: they
"are reverenced like the gods they made.
"Think, if you should prove like one of them,
"what universal fame you would acquire! how
"happy your father! how proud your coun-
"try!"—All this jargon, and a great deal more,
she blundered out, labouring with all her might
to win me over to her opinion. But the greatest part of it has escaped my memory. When

once she had done, thus began the other:
"I, my child, am Learning, not altogether un-
"known to thee. This lady has sufficiently
"enumerated all the blessings of a stone-cutter:
"as such, you will be a mere labourer, and all
"will depend on the sweat of your brow. You
"will lead a poor, illiberal, obscure life, equally
"abject in mind as depressed in body, neither ca-
"pable of assisting your friends, nor able to deter
"your enemies; a low, unenvied drudge, glad
"to truckle to every person of the least eminence,
"dependent on another man's breath, living
"the life of a hare, the property of a gentleman.
"Though you arrive at the excellence of Phi-
"dias or Polycletus, and all men admire your
"workmanship, there is not a single man in his
"senses, who would wish himself to be the work-
"man. However eminent, still you will be a
"mechanick, living from hand to mouth. But,
"if you will be ruled by me, I will make you
"acquainted with the actions and exploits of
"the admired ancients; I will explain to you
"what they have taught, and give you an in-
"sight into all things. Your soul, which is
"your principal part, I will adorn with modera-
"tion,

THE DREAM.

"tion, juſtice, piety, gentleneſs, equity, under-
"ſtanding, firmneſs, the love of virtue, ambi-
"tion of being honourably diſtinguiſhed: theſe
"are the genuine honours of the mind. You
"ſhall know every tranſaction of old, and judge
"of the propriety of what is preſent. I will en-
"able you to ſee into futurity, I will teach you all
"knowledge human and divine. Though you
"are now a poor lad, the ſon of a man who
"would have you be as mean as himſelf, you
"ſhall ſoon become the admiration and envy of
"all men. Your talents will be honoured and
"praiſed by the rich and the great. You ſhall
"have ſuch a robe as mine (which, you ſee, is
"no deſpicable one); you ſhall obtain power
"and pre-eminence. If you ſhould happen to
"go abroad, your fame will go before you. I
"will make you ſo remarkable, that every be-
"holder, jogging his neighbour, ſhall point and
"ſay, [b] *There! that is he!* Whenever any
"matter of conſequence ſhall be debated, re-

[b] Cicero mentions the pride of Demoſthenes on being thus diſtinguiſhed by an old woman carrying water. Tuſcul. Quæſt. B. V. Perſius, Sat. i. Horace, B. IV. Ode iii. Pliny the younger, Book VI. Ep. 6.

" lating

" lating either to individuals, or to the whole
" community, all eyes shall be fixed on you;
" they will be ready with open mouth to swallow
" every word you say, blessing themselves, What
" an orator! what a happy man was the father
" of him! I will bestow on you that immor-
" tality, which is so talked of: when you are
" dead, you shall converse with the wits, and
" keep the very best company. You know what
" a great man Demosthenes became, whose fa-
" ther was nobody: and how Æschines was
" courted by King Philip, though his mother
" was maintained by her timbrel. Socrates was
" at first a statuary, but it was when he knew no
" better; for, when he did, he flew to me, and
" you have heard what reputation he acquired.
" But, if you like to give up such great men,
" such celebrated performances, such elegant
" orations, such fine clothes, honour, glory,
" praise, precedency, power, authority, oratori-
" cal fame, intellectual excellence;—if you are
" determined to forego them all, you must:
" you will be recompensed with an old dirty
" jacket, fit for a slave, and be prepared to
" handle your tools like any other poor, abject,
" down-

" down-looking drudge, with his hammers and
" chifels about him: you muſt never once pre-
" fume to look upwards, left fomething worthy
" of a human creature ſhould happen to engage
" your attention: your whole care will be to
" finiſh every job in a workman-like manner,
" which muſt be always more elegant and better
" attended to than yourfelf, a neglected wretch,
" fcraping a living from duſt and ſtones." I
could forbear no longer, but got up before ſhe
had done ſpeaking, and declared in her favour.
I inſtantly quitted the dirty ſlave, remembering
the whip and the blows, with which I had been
welcomed the day before. With a glad heart I
betook myfelf to Learning. The other, enraged
to be thus deferted, at firſt clinched her fiſt, and
gnaſhed her teeth, with every threat of venge-
ance; but at laſt congealed like Niobe, and became a perfect ſtone. All this may be ſafely believed; for dreams are wonderful things. The
object of my choice, now looking at me, declared ſhe would make me ample fatisfaction
for the equitable decifion I had made. " Do
you fee this chariot? faid ſhe; it is drawn by
winged horfes, like fo many Pegafufes: get into
it,

it, and I will shew you what you had like to have lost." Upon this I got up, and she drove. Being raised aloft, I looked round about me from east to west, beholding cities and nations; and, like Triptolemus [c], scattering something down on the earth. I do not remember at present what it was: I only remember this, that, wherever I came, the people looked up with acclamations, wishing me a good journey, as I flew over their heads. Having shewn me many fine things, and introduced me to much praise, she brought me back again; not in the dress I had set out with, but very fine, I assure you. She then laid hold of my father, who stood expecting me, bade him look at me now, and think of his wise consultation. This is what I saw, while I was hardly more than a child, being disturbed in my sleep, I suppose, by the impression of my uncle's whip.—Here I am interrupted by somebody, who thinks my judicial dream a little of the longest. "But, no doubt, adds another, it was winter, when the nights are long; or, per-

[c] Triptolemus was sent over the world, in a flying chariot, by Ceres, to teach ploughing and sowing. As he flew along, he scattered seed on the ground.

haps,

haps, you were three nights about it, as Jupiter was in begetting Hercules. How came it into the man's head to plague us with his tedious narrative? with the obsolete fooleries of a childish dream? Did he take us for interpreters of his insipid nonsense?" But Xenophon [d], Sir, did not think like you: he related his dream, not as an idle tale of amusement, but as containing something solid and substantial; or he would hardly have taken up his time with it, when surrounded by enemies, and reduced to extremity. For my part, I have related my dream to persuade young men to right courses, especially such as, being disheartened by poverty, might debase their genius by low pursuits. Such will be animated by my example, considering what I originally was, and how I became what I am, not discouraged by the fear of starving; who may venture at least to say this of myself, that I am as well known as the best of the statuaries.

[d] Expedition of Cyrus, Book III.

TIMON:

TIMON:

OR,

THE MAN-HATER.

On the Influence of MONEY.

TIMON:
OR,
THE MAN-HATER.

TIMON.

O JUPITER! the friendly, the hospitable, the sociable, the domestick, the lightning-darting, the oath-observing, the cloud-compelling, the solemn-sounding, and whatever else the brainsick poets please to call thee when they rave in heroicks; for then it is that thou assumest every name, to prop poor desponding metre, and fill up a gap—where is now thy tremendous lightning, thy roaring thunder, thy burning, shining, dreadful bolt? it is now plain that all is a jest, a poetical vapour made up of sounds.

And yet I marvel too how it comes to pass, that those famous arms of thine which kill at any distance—I wonder by what means they have lost their faculty, and are totally out of order: there is not now left a single spark of wrath, to manifest thy indignation against the wicked. There is not a rascal alive that cares one straw for thy thunder, or regards it any more than the wick of an extinguished candle, which might possibly dirty his face indeed, but could not hurt it. Salmoneus has ventured to rival thee in thunder: and why should he not? a man of any spirit may surely defy such a drowsy frozen Jove as thou art. You certainly have been swallowing mandrake [*e*]; you do not see those villains, nor hear those fellows forswearing themselves: you are as blind and as deaf as your great grandfather. Once upon a time, when you were young, and full of spirits, the case was very different: your back was soon up, and woe to those that provoked you. You never gave them a moment's rest; the bolt was in constant practice, the shield

[*e*] Which had the same effect as opium in causing sleep.

was worn without intermission, the thunder roared for ever. Like a shower of darts flew thy skirmishing fire; the earth was shaken and bored like a sieve, mountains of snow and rocks of hail fell about mens' ears: nay, to talk in a higher tone, violent and impetuous were the rains, and every drop a river. No wonder then, that in Deucalion's time, in the twinkling of an eye, the whole world was under water; and every soul must inevitably have perished, had not one little skiff struck upon Mount Lycoris, to preserve the seed of this more rascally generation. But now it is all over with Jupiter: there is not a man that ever sacrifices to you now, or offers you a single garland; except perhaps at the Olympick games, merely to pay respect to an old custom, and not out of any obligation, I assure you. They will soon proceed to play the old game over again, and serve thee like another Saturn. A thousand times already have they robbed thy temple, nor did they stick at falling foul upon thyself in Olympia: meanwhile the sonorous Jupiter was too lazy either to rouse the dogs, or call the neighbours to his assistance; but

fairly

fairly let them escape with their booty. The mighty vanquisher of the giants, the triumphant conqueror of the Titans, with a thunderbolt ten cubits long in his hand, soberly sat still, and let them cut off his locks.— I pray you, good Sir, how long are affairs to go on thus? or when do you intend to be revenged on them? How many Deucalions and Phaëtons, do you think, will be sufficient to restrain such excess of wickedness? for, not to mention other mens concerns, but only to hint at my own, how many of these Athenians have I aggrandised! how many scoundrels, that were not worth a groat, have I enriched! how many beggars have I supported! Have I not spent my whole fortune, to satisfy the desires of my friends? And now, that I am as poor as they were when my bounty found them, my most obedient, devoted, faithful adorers are every man of them ashamed of me, and will not speak to me. If I happen to meet any of them, they pass by me, as they would pass by an old monument not worth regarding. Some of them at a good distance prudently

turn

turn aside and give me the way, not caring to come near any thing so ominous as their old friend and benefactor. Being thus reduced and forlorn, I dig for sixpence [*f*] a day, clad in this miserable garb [*g*]; while, undisturbed by attendants, I moralize over my spade. There is this comfort in my situation, that I do not see the rogues grow fat in their wickedness; for that would be death and fury. But pray be so obliging, thou son of Saturn and Rhea, as to awake (for surely thou hast had a comfortable nap [*h*] of it: Epimenides, who slept seventy-five years together, was nothing to thee).— Awake, I say, and shew thyself a man; blow up the fire of Mount Oeta, and give thy thunderbolt a fresh heat; and, if ever thou didst exert thyself, do it now: unless thou art dead in good earnest, as the Cretans report.

JUPITER.

What fellow is this, Mercury, that I hear thus bawling from Attica? yonder he stands

[*f*] Four oboli. An obolus was something more than five farthings.
[*g*] Διφθέρα, a garment of goat-skin.
[*h*] Hom. Iliad II. verse 2.

by Mount Hymettus, in a miserable garb, dirty and ragged. He seems to be digging; or why does he stoop so? Whoever he is, he is a saucy fellow, I warrant him; some philosopher, I suppose: [i] or he would hardly be so profane.

MERCURY.

What, father, do you not know him? It is Timon of Colyttus, the son of Echechratides. Many a time has he treated us with a feast. You remember—he became suddenly rich, and spent whole hecatombs upon us. I am sure, Sir, we lived like ourselves on your festival days.

JUPITER.

Well! but how came this to pass? He was a gentleman, had a great deal of money, and many friends. How comes he to be in this unseemly situation, delving with a huge spade, and exhibiting all the marks of poverty and wretchedness?

MERCURY.

His good-nature, you must know, and humanity, and pity of all in want, have done his

[i] Ου γαρ αν, suppressa conditione. Vide Hoogeveen de Particulis Græcis, p. 925.

business

business for him. In plain truth, he has been miserably imposed upon. The man had no notion of distinguishing one person from another: all were welcome; and behold the end of it! The more the rooks devoured him, the more they pleased him; as he was convinced, that nothing but stark friendship and pure goodwill could bring them to his table. So, after they had picked his bones clean, and sucked out the marrow, leaving him as dry as a chip [*k*],

[*k*] It may be proper once for all to observe, that, in the style of Lucian, there is often a redundancy of words, as well as a confusion of images. A former translator, having rendered this passage, "And now, after they had stripped him bare "to the bone, and gnawed him, and sucked out all the mar- "row, away they go, and leave him sapless, and cut down to the "very root," observes—that "Lucian passes out of one meta- "phor into another, from that of a body to a tree. Now, "though I will by no means presume to censure this liberty "in so great a master of eloquence as our Author was; yet "one of the nicest criticks France ever bred (I mean Monsieur "St. Evremont) expressly condemns it in his Oeuvres Mêlés, "tom. iv. p. 120. C'est une faute inexcusable de passer d'une "metaphore, par laquelle on auroit commencé, à une nouvelle, "et d'allier ainsi des images qui n'ont nul rapport entre elles. "Quand on est attentif à bien écrire, on scait continuer, et "soutenir la même idée." This modest gentleman brings over a learned Frenchman, to prove what was never denied. A rare example of diffidence in a critick!

they genteelly took their leave, and no longer regarded him. Indeed why should they, since they have no intention of returning his favours? For these reasons, with his spade and his pelt, as you see, he has forsaken the city, being ashamed of living in it any longer. There he is, poor man! turning up the ground for hire; while his breast burns with indignation against the provoking rascals, who, having been enriched by his bounty, now pass scornfully by, and would not know the name of Timon, if they heard it.

JUPITER.

Upon my word, he has reason to be out of humour, and must not be neglected by us. At that rate, we should be as bad as they: if we could forget a man, who has regaled us so often at our altars, with such a number of bulls, and so many of his fattest goats; the smell of which is at this moment in my nostrils. Indeed my time has been so taken up with a parcel of perjured villains, thieves, and robbers; I have been so sweated with those sacrilegious scoundrels, who are so slippery and so numerous, that I have

hardly

hardly had time to close my eyes, or attend to
any thing else: so that it is no wonder I have
not looked down upon Attica this great while.
And then the Philosophers keep such a pother,
with their nonsensical quarrels about empty
words, that actually one cannot hear what other
mortals have to say. Either I must utterly shut up
my ears, or be stunned with the noise they make
about their incorporeal forms, their virtue, and
nobody knows what. It has been owing to such
causes, and not from any want of inclination,
that I have hitherto neglected him. But do you,
Mercury, take Plutus with you, and go to him
directly. Let Plutus take Thesaurus, and let
both take up their abode with Timon, and not
leave him again so readily; though his former
good-natured fit should return, and his charity
induce him to drive them out of doors. As for
those sycophants, I will be revenged on them
for their ingratitude, as soon as I have repaired
my thunderbolt; which I have very much
damaged, in darting too furiously upon Anaxa-
goras the Sophist. He wanted to persuade his
disciples, that we Gods were nobody at all,
forsooth. Unluckily I missed him; for his
friend

friend Pericles put his hand between us: so the bolt fell upon the Temple of Castor and Pollux, and, in destroying that, was almost destroyed itself; it went with such violence against the hard stones. Though I believe it will be a sufficient plague to them, to see Timon rich again.

MERCURY.

To make a noise, to be impudent, and importunate, I find, is useful to others, as well as the wranglers at the bar! Behold, here is a poor fellow going to be suddenly enriched, because he has given himself airs, and been so clamorous, that Jupiter is almost stunned with his bawling! who, had he been contented to dig in silence, might have dug his heart out, before Jove would have shewn him the least regard!

PLUTUS.

Positively, I will go no more near him.

JUPITER.

No! not when I command you, Sir?

PLUTUS.

Upon my word, he has used me extremely ill: he scattered me piecemeal, he kicked me out;

out; when I was his very beft friend. He even fhook me off, as if he had burnt his fingers with handling me. Would you have me go to him again, to be fquandered amongft parafites, flatterers, and harlots? I beg, Jupiter, that you will fend me to fuch as know the value of me, and will entertain me accordingly. Such never think they can have too much of my company. As for the fools, that could make ducks and drakes of their money, let them even have enough of their dearly-beloved poverty, and be bleffed with a fpade, a leathern jacket, and fixpence a day!

JUPITER.

Timon will play you no fuch tricks for the future: his fpade has tutored him fufficiently. If there be any feeling in him, I warrant you, he will never more prefer poverty to riches. Indeed, you feem to be always grumbling: why fhould you find fault with Timon for fetting the door open, and giving you leave to do as you would? He never baulked you in any expedition, nor had he the leaft jealoufy of you. I have

have known the time when you have complained
lustily of the rich, for setting their seal upon you,
and confining you, as they are apt to do, with
bolts and bars. You said, it was impossible for
you to enjoy a glimpse of light, shut up in such
miserable servitude, under lock and key. You
complained of being stifled in darkness, which
made you look so pale and so sickly. You said,
your constitution was devoured by continual
anxiety; that you had lost the right use of your
fingers by continually scraping money together;
and that you only wanted an opportunity to
make your escape. In short, you thought it a
terrible thing, to be kept untouched, like the
virgin Danaë, in a brazen or iron closet, and
tutored by the rigorous care of interest and
arithmetick. You wondered why they should
be so unaccountably fond of you, since they
had not the heart to enjoy you when they
might; but were always upon the watch, with
their eyes perpetually on the hinge or the key-
hole; thinking it quite sufficient to have barely
the power of using you, and preventing any
body else; like the dog in the manger. You
thought them very ridiculous, who were always
pinching

pinching and hoarding, and jealous of even their own guts; not considering that some rascally footman, or butler, or puppy of a tutor, would come flily upon the odious wretch of a master, and, sneaking off with his money, leave him to meditate alone, over his glimmering, twinkling, starvling rush-light.—What method of proceeding is this? You are neither satisfied the one way nor the other.

PLUTUS.

If you will be pleased to consider the matter, I fancy you will find that I have not done any thing without reason. That easiness and mildness of Timon's government was not in reality out of good-will to me. And as to those who locked me up in the dark, that I might grow fat and well-liking, meanwhile they never laid finger on me, nor suffered any one to see me, I looked on them to be out of their senses, cruel villains who could suffer me to rot in a jail without why or wherefore; never considering how soon they must go and leave me to the possession of some other of Fortune's favourites.

'rites. I neither like the one, nor the other; neither Timon, nor his oppofite. They are moſt to my mind, who neither hoard me up to no purpoſe, nor ſcatter me to as little; but make a moderate uſe of me. Put the caſe thus, good Jupiter: ſuppoſe a man was to marry a handſome young wife, and afterwards take no account of her conduct; ſuffer her to go and come whenever ſhe likes, by night or day; contentedly permit her to keep whatever company ſhe will; nay, even open his doors for the reception of gallants, and invite all the neighbouring cuckold-makers;—can ſuch a man have any love for his wife? I think, Jupiter knows better. On the contrary, if a man marries a fine young lady, for the ſake of having children, and afterwards will not ſo much as touch her, nor allow any body to look at her, ſuffering her youth to waſte away in hopeleſs virginity, and all this under a pretence of ſuperabundant fondneſs, while he ſtalks about with his eyes ſunk in his head, as pale and as lean as the moſt ardent lover; is ſuch a man to be reckoned in his ſober ſenſes; who, when he ought to be purſuing every delightful purpoſe

of

of wedlock, suffers a lovely young woman to languish out a forlorn life, as if she was in training for a priestess of Ceres [1]? It goes to my heart, I assure you, to be kicked about, consumed, and devoured, by heedless spendthrifts: nor, on the other hand, can I brook being kept in fetters, like a branded runaway slave.

JUPITER.

However, you may rest yourself satisfied; for they are both of them sufficiently punished: these, while, like Tantalus, they neither eat nor drink, gaping only with dry chops after gold; and those, while, as Phineus was served by the harpies, their parasites eat the meat out of their mouths. But go; get you gone: you will find Timon much wiser than he has been.

PLUTUS.

Impossible! He will let me out of his coffers before I have rested a moment; he is so

---

[1] This passage had like to have occasioned an unhappy quarrel amongst the Learned. While some doubted whether Ceres ever had a priestess; others more stoutly argued that she had many, vindicating the honours of the Goddess with a becoming acrimony. See Moses du Soul.

terribly afraid of being overwhelmed with riches. I might just as wisely think of filling the sieves of the Belides, while the water runs faster out than in: so free an egress is always open to his profusion.

JUPITER.

If then he does not stop up the vent, you will soon make your escape again, kindly leaving him his hairy doublet and his spade at the bottom of the vessel. However, go; and let him be rich. And remember, Mercury, as you come back, to call at Ætna, and bring a blacksmith or two to sharpen my thunderbolt; for I see I shall want to have it in good order.

MERCURY.

Come, Plutus; come along. Hey-day! what is the matter? What, do you limp? I knew you were blind; but never dreamed of your being lame too.

PLUTUS.

I am never so, except when I am sent on an errand by Jupiter; when I immediately become unaccountably lame of both my feet, so that

it

it is with great difficulty I reach the end of my journey: meanwhile the poor fellow, who expected me, is grown an old man. But when I am to take my leave, I am swifter than any of the feathered kind. The race is no sooner begun, than I am declared the winner: I take such strides, and run so fast, the eye can scarcely keep up with me.

MERCURY.

I know not how to believe you now; for I could name some hundreds of my acquaintance as rich as Crœsus all on a sudden, who but the other day could not have mustered a penny to purchase a halter; fine fellows, who to-day are pompously drawn by white horses, and who yesterday would have given their ears for the conveniency of bestriding a jack-ass. They strut about with their purple and rings, and, I really believe, have some doubt whether they have not dreamed themselves into all this wealth.

PLUTUS.

What you say, Mercury, is nothing to the purpose. I do not go to such persons on my own

own feet, nor am I sent to them by Jupiter, but by Pluto, who is famous for bestowing riches, as his very name denotes. When I am to pass from one to another, they cram me into a will, and sealing me carefully up, carry me off in a bundle; while the testator lies dead in some dark corner of the house, tucked up in an old piece of linen, for the cats to fight about. Those, who thought themselves sure of having me, stand in the market in expectation as earnest as that of the young swallow waiting the return of the old one. But when at last the seal is broken, and the will opened, and my new Lord's name declared, who is commonly some worthless cousin, some mean sycophant, or prostitute slave; immediately my alert gentleman, by dint of his newly-acquired possessions, the reward of his past services, forgets that he ever had been Pyrrhias [k], or Dromo [k], or Tibias [k]; and, for the future, is to be saluted by the name of Megacles [l], or Megabyzus [l], or Protarchus [l]. As looks the fisherman, when a huge fish, after swallow-

[k] Usual names of slaves.
[l] Names of great men.

ing all his bait, breaks out of the net, and bids farewel; so look the disappointed expectants one at another, for ever out of all chance of obtaining the prize. This silly fellow, an entire stranger to all elegance of manners, running headlong upon a heap of money, though he still remembers the fetters, and has not forgot the smack of a whip, pricking up his ears as it passes; to whom a temple and a house of correction are objects of equal awe;—this fellow grows intolerable to all manner of persons; abuses his betters; and beats his brother slaves, to practise his whip-hand. He presently takes to harlots and horses [*m*]; falls into the hands of pimps and parasites, who swear he is one of the most accomplished characters of the age, much handsomer than Nireus, of a better family than Cecrops or Codrus, wiser than Ulysses, a thousand times richer than Crœsus; when,

---

[*m*] Very few of the Athenians had a fortune sufficient to keep race-horses. A young rake in Aristophanes had run his father in debt twelve minæ, equivalent to 38 *l.* 15 *s.* of our money, for the purchase of his steed, κοππαλιας. Brumoy says, that the worst thing these frugal Republicans wished to their enemies, was, that they might keep fine horses. Theatre des Grecs, t. v. p. 481.

in the twinkling of an eye, he fools away what had been scraped together with all the pains and cares of perjury, fraud, and rapine.

MERCURY.

What you observe is very just. But when you walk on your own legs, as you are blind, how do you find the way? How do you distinguish those who deserve your favours, to whom Jupiter sends you?

PLUTUS.

You do not imagine that I ever find those I am sent to!

MERCURY.

Truly I believe not: or you could never have passed by Aristides, to make a visit to Hipponicus, and Callias, and many more rascals in the town not worth hanging. But how do you generally proceed in your expeditions?

PLUTUS.

I wander up and down till somebody happens to lay hold of me. Whoever is so happy hugs me close, and offers you a thanksgiving for such unexpected good luck.

MERCURY.

MERCURY.

Is not Jupiter then mightily mistaken, who imagines that you really enrich such as he thinks deserving?

PLUTUS.

He may well miss of his aim, who, knowing me to be blind, sends me to seek out a needle in a bottle of hay; which those that see the best could never find. Indeed honesty is so very rare, and rascals are so many and so ravenous, that it is no wonder they generally secure me.

MERCURY.

Well, but when you forsake them, as you know not a foot of the way, how is it that you are so very expeditious?

PLUTUS.

On these occasions I have always the perfect use of my eyes, and feet too.

MERCURY.

Answer me this too: I pray, since your eyes are so bad (I beg pardon for my freedom), and you are so ill-looking, and so lame; how comes it that you have so many lovers, and are so universally admired? Whoever obtains your favours is superlatively happy; but to him whom you slight life becomes a burden. Nay, I myself have known several so wretchedly infatuated with your charms, that, in a fit of despair, they have not scrupled to jump headlong from a rock into the sea. You must yourself confess, I think, that such persons are mad.

PLUTUS.

Do you think they see me as I really am, with all my imperfections about me?

MERCURY.

Do they not? or are they as blind as you?

PLUTUS.

It is not blindness, Sir, but ignorance and error, which are now so universally predominant, that darken their understandings. Besides, notwithstanding this deformity, I can put on a good face; and, when they see me with such fine clothes, so much gold, and so many jewels; thinking it all beauty without paint, they fall over head and ears in love, and die to obtain me:
when,

when, if any one should unmask me, and discover me to them in my genuine nakedness, no doubt, they would upbraid their own stupid brains, for blindly dreaming of any thing desirable in me.

MERCURY.

But, when a man is really become rich, and wears himself the mask which you mention, he is not mistaken in it then. And yet, you see, he would sooner part with his head than his money; when it is impossible but he must know how the case is.

PLUTUS.

Many things contribute towards maintaining the cheat.

MERCURY,

Explain,

PLUTUS.

When a man first throws open his doors to admit my visit, Pride, Folly, Ostentation, Effeminacy, Insolence, Deceit, and twenty more of the same kind, steal slily in along with me. When once

once these have taken possession of the mind, a man admires what he ought to abhor, and greedily pursues what he ought to avoid. He so dotes on me, who introduced, and am thus attended by these my guards; that, sooner than part with me, he would suffer every extremity.

MERCURY.

Indeed, Plutus, you are wonderfully smooth, and slippery, and fickle, and hard to hold, having no handle that one can trust to: you slip, one knows not how, like an eel, through one's fingers. But poverty on the contrary sticks like birdlime, easily caught indeed: it is all over tenterhooks, touch and take, it holds you fast. But while we are thus trifling, we neglect an important affair.

PLUTUS.

What is that?

MERCURY.

We have not brought with us Thesaurus, who is most wanted.

PLUTUS,

PLUTUS.

Do not be concerned about that. When I come up to you gentlemen above, I always leave him below with the doors bolted, and give him strict charge not to open till he hears my voice.

MERCURY.

Come then, let us be going to Attica. Do you lay hold of a lappet of my cloak, and stick close till we get to the end of our journey.

PLUTUS.

You are in the right to lead me; for, if I was left to myself, I might stumble upon Hyperbolus or Cleon. But what noise is this? It is like iron struck upon stone.

MERCURY.

It is Timon, but a little way off, working with his spade in the gravelly soil. Bless me! there is Poverty, and Labour, and Strength, and Wisdom, and Fortitude, the whole regiment of Hunger, more respectable guards than those of Plutus!

PLUTUS.

PLUTUS.

Let us be gone, Mercury, immediately: we shall never make any thing of him, with such an army about him.

MERCURY.

Let us not be disheartened: you know what Jupiter said.

POVERTY.

Whither are you conducting *him*, you murderer of Argus [n]?

MERCURY.

We are dispatched by Jupiter to Timon.

POVERTY.

He was in a fine pickle when I undertook him, ruined by Luxury. But, recommending him to Wisdom and Labour, I have made a man of him. And will Plutus go to him again? am I so despicable, so fit to be trampled on? and would you deprive me of him, my sole pos-

---

[n] Argus, having a hundred eyes, was ordered by Juno to preserve the fair Io inviolate. It is no reflection on him, that he did not succeed.

session,

fession, whom I have so carefully accomplished in virtue? would Plutus again give him up to Insolence and Pride, and make him the silly fop he was before? And, when every thing valuable is gone, will he then again give him to me?

MERCURY.

Jupiter will have it so.

POVERTY.

I go then. Come along, Labour, and Wisdom, and all my companions. Timon shall soon have reason to remember how good a friend I have been to him, who must now leave him; how well I have assisted him, and in what interesting studies I have engaged him. As long as he was connected with me, his body was healthy, and his mind vigorous; he led the life of a man, and minded the things that concerned him; nor did he ever lay claim to the superfluities which did not belong to him.

MERCURY.

They are marching off: let us go up to him.

TIMON.

TIMON.

What villains are you? what business have you here, to disturb a poor labouring man? But I will make you repent it, abominable scoundrels as you are; unless you like to be well pelted with clods and stones.

MERCURY.

Do not, pray, do not! We are not men, Timon: I am Mercury, and this gentleman is Plutus. Jupiter has sent us to you, in consequence of your prayers. So give over your work, take plenty of money, and much good may it do you!

TIMON.

Be gods with all my heart! that shall not save your bacon. I hate you all alike. And as for this blinking rascal here, let him be who he will, he shall have my spade in his guts, depend upon it.

PLUTUS.

Let us go pr'ythee, Mercury: this fellow is as mad as a march hare, and will certainly do me a mischief.

MERCURY.

MERCURY.

Be not so boorish, Timon. Lay aside thy rusticity, and welcome thy good fortune. Once again be rich, be the great man of Athens, be alone happy, and despise the ungrateful.

TIMON.

I ask you no favour; only do not be troublesome. My spade is my estate; and I am very happy, provided nobody comes near me.

MERCURY.

How unaccountable!
" And I must bear these big resolves to Jove [m]!" You might be expected indeed not to be overfond of mankind, you have not been over-well used by them: but to hate the gods, who take such care of you, is unpardonable.

TIMON.

Believe me, Mercury, I take very kindly this favour that Jupiter and you intended me. But as for Plutus, I am determined to have nothing more to do with him.

[m] Hom. Il. xv. ver. 202.

MERCURY.

MERCURY.

But why, Timon?

TIMON.

Why! because he has done me unspeakable mischief, betraying me to flatterers, and exposing me to such as would have cut my throat; making me odious and abhorred, destroying my health and morals with debauchery, and pointing me out as a mark for envy. Last of all, having had his ends of me, he treacherously left me in the lurch. Poverty, on the contrary, by accustoming me to manly exercises, to honesty and truth, has supplied me with all I wanted, and taught me, contentedly labouring for my bread, to laugh at all the world thinks valuable. Poverty taught me, that my happiness was to be found within my own breast; that there only I might enjoy the riches, which neither the artifice of flattery, the threats of falshood, the rage of the populace, the tumult of elections, nor the plots of tyranny, could ever rob me of. Being therefore made strong by labour, I diligently cultivate this little spot; and, while I behold not the iniquities of the city,

city, my spade amply supplies every wish of my heart. So, Mercury, I would have you go back, and take your companion with you. I shall be perfectly satisfied, if Jupiter will but furnish every moment of every man's life with sufficient cause of lamentation.

MERCURY.

But why so? it is not proper that all men should lament.—But have done with this pettish childish talk, and give a welcome to Plutus. The gifts of Jupiter are not to be treated thus.

PLUTUS.

Will you only hear, Timon, what I have to say for myself? or will you take it ill, if I speak?

TIMON.

To oblige this gentleman, I will hear what you can say. But none of your tedious nonsensical circumlocutions, pr'ythee now! I like not your provoking speech-makers, not I!

PLUTUS.

I might have expected your permission to say a good deal on so copious a subject; for you have

have not been sparing of accusations. But
weigh the matter fairly, and then see if ever I
did you harm. It is true, I was the means of
all your pleasure, of all your honours. It was
I that wove your garlands, and was the minister
of joy. By my means it was, that all eyes were
fixed on you, all talked of you, all coveted your
company. If your flatterers injured you, am I
to be blamed for that? I have much more reason
to blame you, for throwing me so shamefully
away upon such unsufferable rascals, who
bewitched you with their praises, and practised
every sneaking art to obtain me. Your accusation
of treachery in deserting you, may very
fairly be retorted on yourself, who kicked me
neck and heels out of your house. When behold!
instead of the fine cloak you had been
used to, your beloved Poverty arrayed you in
her hairy doublet! Mercury is my witness, how
I begged and prayed of Jupiter not to send me
to you. For I knew what I had to expect.

MERCURY.

But observe! Plutus, he is now quite another
thing. Do not be backward. Do you, Timon,
dig

dig on. And do you, Plutus, convey Thesaurus under the spade. He will attend to your call.

TIMON.

Well, if I must be rich again, I must. There is no contending against the Gods. But alas! alas! into what trouble and vexation are you plunging a poor fellow, who was very happy, and did nothing in the world to deserve being tormented all at once with so much money!

MERCURY.

I beg you will bear with this heavy grievance, as well as you can; that your former flatterers may burst with envy. I shall fly back over Ætna to Heaven.

PLUTUS.

He flutters his wings, and is gone. Do you stay here, till I go and send Thesaurus. But strike harder. I charge you, Thesaurus, to be at his bidding, and put yourself in the way of his spade. Dig deeper, Timon. I leave you.

TIMON.

Come then, my trusty spade, let me see what thou canst do towards digging up Thesaurus

into day-light! O Jupiter, the miracle-monger!
O Mercury, the gold-finder! and the friendly
Corybantes! whence in the name of wonder
comes all this money? I am afraid I am dreaming;
and that, when I wake, it will prove to
be coals. It is real coin, in good troth! fine,
blushing, weighty metal, doing one's eyes good
to behold it! [*n*] O gold! how desirable art
thou to mortals [*o*]! Thou shinest brighter than
a warm fire, and shinest night and day! Come,
my precious, my dearest, come! Now I believe
that Jupiter transformed himself to gold! What
fair virgin would not with open arms receive
so brisk a lover jumping through the tiles?
Midas and Crœsus, what are you to Timon? All
the wealth of Delphi a mere nothing in comparison
of mine! nor is any eastern king of them
all a match for me! My dear spade, my beloved
jacket, you may now keep holiday: I will
hang you up as an offering to Pan [*p*]. As for
myself, when I have purchased me a piece of
ground in a remote corner, and built me a castle

[*n*] Ω χρυσε, δεξιωμα καλλιστον βροτοις. Euripides.
[*o*] Διδομεν γαρ πυρ οτι διαφερτης.
       Pindar. Hymn. Ol. 1.
[*p*] Under whose protection he had lately been.

upon it, to guard my money and myself alone, there will I live, and there will I be buried. For the remainder of my life, know all men by these presents, that I am resolved to fly from, forget, and despise them all! Tell me of friendship, or hospitality, or society, or pity! it is all a jest! to compassionate the afflicted, to succour the distressed, is a heinous transgression, the bane of morality! Happy wolves [*q*], who live alone! Timon is resolved, like you, to think himself his only friend, hating and detesting all others, as so many implacable enemies, or insidious assassins. Accordingly to converse with any one of them, I will think an abomination; nay, should I look at any one, accursed be the day! In all respects they shall be no more to me than so many stocks or stones; I will neither receive any message from, nor make any bargain with, them. Solitude shall be the guardian of my peace! Relations, companions, countrymen, and all the rest, insipid nonsense! the affectation of fools! Let Timon alone be rich, despising all others!

[*q*] Μόνηες διαίτα. These two words tempted Tiberius Hempsterhusius to be witty. Tiberius declares, though a very grave man, that wolves are a species of monks.

let Timon revel by himself, not pestered with
flattery, not loaded with praise! let him sacrifice,
let him feast alone; and, shaking off all others,
be neighbour and guest to himself! On every occasion, let him love, and associate with, only himself; and, if he must die, let him put on his garland [r] himself! May he ever cherish that most
precious name, Timon the Man-hater! may
moroseness, ill-nature, pride, perverseness, in-
humanity, sullenness, superciliousness, and ill-
breeding, characterize my favourite manners! If
I shall happen to see a man burning in the fire,
and begging one, for heaven's sake, to relieve
him, I will quench it by pouring in pitch and
oil. If a poor fellow has been overtaken by a
torrent, and holds out a hand for me to save
him, I shall be sure to push him in over head
and ears. In this manner am I resolved to be
even with mankind. This is the law of Timon,
the son of Echechratides, the Colyttean, proposed, carried, and confirmed by himself; and
which he himself will ever maintain! I would

[r] Those, who had run the race of life, were crowned
as conquerors. The custom still prevails. See Lettres sur
la Grece, par Monsieur Guys.

give

give a good deal, that all the world knew how
rich I am: I am sure they could not fail to
hang themselves. But heyday! what is the
matter here? swarms of dusty fellows on all
sides of me puffing and blowing—I fancy they
smell the gold. I have a good mind to get up
upon this bank, that I may pelt them the better with stones—No—I will break my law for
once—I will do myself the pleasure of speaking to them, that my contempt of them may
cut their very souls. That, I think, will be best.
So I will stay here to receive them. So! who
is this that comes first? Gnathonides the parasite—He lately offered me a halter, civil gentleman! when I begged something of him to buy
a supper. The rascal ere now has swilled many
a hogshead of my wine. However, I am glad
to see him the very first man: he shall hang
his lip presently, I warrant him.

GNATHONIDES.

I said the Gods could never long neglect so
worthy a gentleman! the handsome, good-natured, generous, jovial Timon! Sir, I am your
most obedient servant.

TIMON,

TIMON.

What? the moft rapacious of all vultures! the greateft villain upon earth! Sir, your's!

GNATHONIDES.

Still the fame, I fee—witty, fond of a joke—But where fhall we be jolly together? I have juft got one of the rareft catches you ever heard: I will fing it to you.

TIMON.

With this fpade I will teach you the fineft elegy in the world, fo pathetick, fo—

GNATHONIDES.

What now? Surely you do not ftrike me? O dear! O dear! O dear!—he has wounded me fadly. Bear witnefs—you fhall appear at Areopagus [1] for this.

TIMON.

Stay one moment longer, and you may lay your indictment for murder. For as fure as—

[1] A court of juftice at Athens.

GNATHO-

GNATHONIDES.

No, no—But pray now apply a little gold to the wound: I have heard it is the best thing in the world for stopping of blood.

TIMON.

Are you not gone?

GNATHONIDES.

I am going. Plague take you! what an alteration here is indeed!

TIMON.

But what bald-pated fellow is this that comes now? Philiades, the most execrable of all hypocrites! This honest man had a whole farm of me, besides [*t*] two talents for his daughter's portion, for praising my singing. When nobody else had the assurance to say a word, he swore my note was sweeter than that of a dying swan. But, when I was lately taken ill, and thought he could not do less than afford me every kind office, behold! my gentleman hit me a slap in the face, for presuming to expect it.

[*t*] 317 *l*. 13 *s*.

PHILIADES.

What impudence! Now, I suppose, you know Timon! Gnathonides now forsooth vouchsafes a visit! he is rightly served, and no otherwise than such a fellow deserves. It is for us, who have been his old friends and companions, to pretend to speak to Timon; and not for such upstarts as he is. And yet I would not intrude neither. My worthy Sir, I hope I see you well. You observe these faithless parasites, true ravens, never present but when there is picking! there is no putting trust in man, as the world goes now-a-days. Vice and ingratitude rule the roast! As I was coming along, bringing a talent, for your honour's necessary occasions, I was agreeably surprized with the news of your sudden and vast riches. However, as I was almost here, I took the liberty of coming on, just to hint to your honour what you have to trust to amongst men. Not that a gentleman of your understanding needs to be told any thing, who might very well have been privy counsellor to Nestor himself.

TIMON.

TIMON.

To be sure, Sir! But approach a little nearer, Philiades. Let me just salute you with my spade, for the sake of old acquaintance.

PHILIADES.

The ungrateful monster has fractured my skull, I really believe; purely for offering my friendly advice.

TIMON.

The third man that comes is Demeas the orator, a precious scoundrel! He has a decree in his hand, and pretends to be my relation, forsooth. This fellow had been fined sixteen talents, and was in jail for the debt, which, out of compassion, I paid for him, and set him at liberty. Afterwards, when he happened to have the distribution of the money [*u*] for the tribe

---

[*u*] Two or three oboli used to be given to every Athenian, to encourage his attendance on publick occasions. Pericles is said to have been the first author of this institution, for which he was greatly censured by his wise and virtuous countrymen, who foresaw the effects it would have. Josephus the Historian, without intending any compliment, ascribes the invention of money to Cain.

of Erechtheis, I came to him, and begged of him to give me what fell to my share. But truly he was in doubt of my being a citizen.

DEMEAS.

Hail! Timon, ornament of thy race, pillar of Athens, bulwark of Greece! the people in full convocation, and [w] both the courts await your orders! But, in the first place, be pleased to hear the bill, which I have got passed in your favour: "Whereas Timon, the son of Eche-
"chratides of Colyttus, not only remarkable
"for his virtue and honour, but a man of such
"exalted wisdom, as is not to be paralleled in
"Greece, has never ceased through his whole
"life to confer extraordinary favours on the
"commonwealth, hath come off victorious in
"boxing, wrestling, and running at the Olym-
"pick games, all in one day; besides the
"Chariot race—"

TIMON.

Why, man, I never saw the Olympick games in my life.

[w]. The Senate of the five hundred, and the Court of Areopagus. See Potter's Antiquities.

DEMEAS.

DEMEAS.

Pshaw! what signifies that? you will see them some time or other. I must go by the form—" performed wonderful feats of prowess " last year at Acharnæ, and cut to pieces two " divisions of the Peloponnesians—"

TIMON.

How? I never bore arms in my life! I never served upon any expedition in my born days!

DEMEAS.

Merit is always modest. But ill it would become us to forget yours.—" In passing laws, " in councils, and in the field, hath rendered " signal service to the city: for these and sun- " dry other causes them thereunto moving, it " hath seemed good to the Senate and people, " to the publick in general, and every indi- " vidual in particular, to erect a golden statue " of Timon in the citadel, as near as may be " to Minerva, grasping a thunderbolt in his " right-hand, and having his head surrounded " with rays; that he be crowned with seven " golden crowns, as is to be proclaimed this
" feast

"feast of Bacchus (for on Timon's account it
"is kept this day). This decree was pro-
"nounced by Demeas the orator, the near re-
"lation and disciple of Timon, of Timon who
"excels in oratory, as in every thing else which
"he is pleased to undertake." Such is the
decree. I could have wished for the honour
of introducing my son to you, whom I have presumed to call by your name.

TIMON.

This is absolutely the first time that I have
heard of your being married.

DEMEAS.

I hope to be married the next year, which
will be just as well. And, as soon as Providence shall have crowned my conjugal endear-
ments with a male child, I will certainly name
him Timon.

TIMON.

There! take that! Now what do you think
of marrying?

DEMEAS.

DEMEAS.

What now? Oh dear! oh! do you set up for a tyrant? dares such a fellow as you, an alien, presume to strike a gentleman? But you shall be brought before your betters, for setting the citadel on fire, and for many other crimes, which you have committed.

TIMON.

But the citadel has not been set on fire: there you lie.

DEMEAS.

But you have enriched yourself by breaking into the treasury.

TIMON.

But it has not been broken into: there again you lie.

DEMEAS.

It will be by and by. Though indeed you have all the riches of it already.

TIMON.

Take another blow then!

DEMEAS.

DEMEAS.

Oh my back! my back!

TIMON.

Come, make no noise, unless you want another of the same sort. It would be a great shame truly, if I, who, unarmed, cut in pieces two divisions of the Lacedæmonians, could not break the bones of one poor rascal. I should be very little the better man at that rate for my boxing, and wrestling, for my victories at the Olympick games?—But what now? who comes here? Thrasycles the Philosopher? The very man! Here he comes, hanging his enormous beard, bristling up his eye-brows, muttering some mighty matter to himself, looking as gruff as you please, with his hair standing up, in short another Boreas, such as you see puffing and swelling his cheeks on the northern edge of an old map. This man, whose dress and demeanour are so decent and modest, who is so grave and so wise, in a morning will run you over twenty fine speeches, in praise of Piety, and Virtue, and Moderation; most devoutly censuring all those who tread the slippery paths

of Pleasure. But when he comes from the
bath to a good supper, and the servant has supplied him with a plentiful cup of good wine,
which he hates to adulterate with water; the
delicious Lethe quickly makes him forget the
sober documents of the morning, and Thrasycles
can be as jovial as the best of them. Voracious
as a kite, his busy arms defend the dish, while,
bending over it, his beard streaming with
gravy, he gulps like a half-starved hound, expecting no doubt to swallow his celebrated Virtue in the last remaining mouthful of some relishing bit. And, though that industrious
finger of his permits no savoury sediment to
lurk in the dish, yet is he perpetually grumbling,
as if he had reason to complain of his share;
though he has secured all the pastry [x], with the
entire boar [x]. After so much cramming, he
gets drunk, dances, sings, swears, and quarrels.
Meanwhile every bumper is prefaced with a
panegyrick on temperance and sobriety, stammered out as well as drunken philosophy will
allow. Next begins the operation of his eme-

[x] The Guests were accustomed to carry home with
them the remains of a feast.

ticks,

ticks, last of all they carry him off, clinging with both his hands to a wench. When this man is sober, I defy any one to go beyond him, in lying, impudence, or avarice. He can tickle your vanity so rarely, forswear himself so readily, and impose upon you with so grave a face, as is not any where to be equalled. In short, he is a finished piece, nicely touched off, and perfectly fine. Yet perhaps the good creature can howl a little.—What, Thrasycles! I have impatiently expected this favour.

THRASYCLES.

I do not come, good Sir, believe me, for the same reason that others do, who, knowing you to be an honest open-hearted unsuspecting man, expect, by dint of a flattering speech, to get from you your money or your supper. Timon needs not be told how little I esteem what is called good living. The simplest of all foods, a little cresses, a little thyme, contents me: except when I have a mind to regale; for then I add a little salt. My drink comes from the clear fountain. And this old cloak is more to my satisfaction than the finest purple. As for
gold,

gold, I value it no more than the meanest pebble. Far be it from me to esteem such transitory vanities! It was on your account, it was for your advantage, that I came hither, hearing of your dangerous situation in the midst of most treacherous, most destructive riches, the cause of unspeakable mischief. If you take my advice, you will throw all your money into the sea; for, sure I am, a good man, who knows the value of philosophy, can have no occasion for any other wealth. Or, suppose you just step gently in up to the middle, and drop your bags quietly into the shallow water, while there is nobody to see you besides me your friend. Or, if you do not so well approve of that, you may toss your money out of the house in parcels, and in sums proportioned to the respective occasions of all in want. I would not have you reserve a single obolus to yourself. But doubtless, while you thus distribute it, if a philosopher should come in the way, he would have a double or treble share, as it is most fitting. Not that I —— Heaven forbid that I should desire any! Though, to be sure, if I had a little, I could do good with it amongst my friends.

friends. This wallet of mine does not hold quite two Ægina bushels [y]. If you would be so good as just to fill it for me, I should be satisfied. For a philosopher ought to be contented with a little, and not extend his desires beyond his wallet.

TIMON.

You are most undoubtedly in the right: I cannot but commend what you say, friend Thrasycles. So, if you please, before I fill your wallet, I will just take measure of your head with my spade, that I may match it with many a hearty bang.

THRASYCLES.

Here is fine work! what will this world come to? Where are your laws and your liberty, if an honest man is to be thus beaten by a vile ruffian?

TIMON.

My good Thrasycles, do not be angry; I scorn to cheat you. Rather than you should

[y] The medimnus or bushel of Athens contained 4 pecks 6 pints 3,501 solid inches. That of Ægina was much larger.

complain,

complain, I will give you over-meafure.—Heaven and Earth! what a rabble is here! Blepſias, and Laches, and Gniphon, and a whole army, who ſhall every man of them repent of his viſit. But my poor ſpade muſt have a little reſt: it has had hard duty. I will even get up upon this rock, and ply the dogs with a ſhower of ſtones.

BLEPSIAS.

Forbear! forbear! we are all going.

TIMON.

Not without loſing a little blood [z], I believe.

[z] The victorious Timon inſinuates his claim to a triumph, which was not granted for what the Greeks called ἀναιμακτὶ νικᾶν, *incruenta victoria*, a victory obtained without blood.

CHARON:

OR,

THE OBSERVERS.

On the Vanity of HUMAN LIFE.

CHARON:

OR,

THE OBSERVERS.

MERCURY and CHARON.

MERCURY.

WHY so merry, Charon? Pray what is the meaning of thus leaving your vessel and coming up hither? You did not use to mind matters above ground.

CHARON.

I longed to see how affairs go on in this world, what men are doing in it, and what it is that they so lament the loss of, when they come down to us. For not a soul of them ever steps into my boat without tears. I therefore afked leave of Pluto to quit my employment, and, like the young Theffalian [a], fpend one day above ground. And I think I have been very lucky to meet with you, who are fo well acquainted here; and who, I am fure, as I am a ftranger, will go about with me, and fhew me every thing.

MERCURY.

I have not time, Mr. Ferryman. I am going about fome bufinefs relating to mortals, which the fupreme Jupiter has fet me upon. You know very well how little a matter makes him angry. If he fhould catch me loitering away my time, he may take it into his head to confine me conftantly amongft you in darknefs. Or, he may poffibly ferve me as he did [b] Vulcan not long ago, take me by a foot, and tofs me out of Heaven; that the poor Blackfmith may not be the only limping waiter for the Gods to laugh at.

CHARON.

And can you leave your old comrade, companion, and fhip-mate, to fhift for himfelf in a

[a] Protefilaus.
[b] Hom. Il. i. ver. 590.

ftrange

strange place? would you suffer me to wander about at random by myself upon earth, where I know nobody? Pray remember, O son of Maia, that I never once desired you to strike a stroke at either the pump or the oar. With those broad shoulders of yours, you lie stretched at your length, snoring on the deck: except when you can find some talkative ghost, to gossip with all the way. Old as I am, I am obliged to manage the two oars myself, without any assistance from you. But, for your father's sake, my dear little Mercury, do not leave me so! Shew me what is to be seen in human life; that, when I go back, I may have something to say. If you leave me, I shall be never the better for coming. As a blind man staggers in the dark, so shall I blunder in the light. Do, my dear Cyllenius, go with me; I will remember your kindness as long as I live.

MERCURY.

I shall be well beaten, I see plainly, on this occasion: my complaisance in accompanying you will be rewarded with a good drubbing. But what can one do? There is no holding out
against

against the importunities of a friend. But as to your seeing every thing particularly, that, my good Sir, is impracticable. For it would require your living here many years. The consequence of which would be, I should be advertised by Jupiter, as a deserter; and you, by neglecting your works of death, and conveying no ghosts for so long a time, would grievously injure the empire of Pluto. Æacus too the Toll-gatherer would be plaguily vexed at not earning a single obolus. Our business therefore is, to consult on the best method for you to obtain a general view of the principal things.

CHARON.

You are the best judge how to proceed: I can say nothing to it, being an entire stranger.

MERCURY.

We must get upon some eminence, from whence you may have a prospect all round you. I wish you could get up into Heaven: then I should be easy. For that would be high enough in all conscience to see any thing from. But since you, the constant associate of murky ghosts,

ghosts, must not set a foot on the threshold of Jove, we must look out for a hill high enough for our purpose.

CHARON.

You know in what manner I am used to talk to you in our voyage over the Styx. When the wind is contrary, and the waves run high, you, who know nothing at all of the matter, are for having me to furl my sail, or let go the bowline, or run right before the wind; but I always tell you, your only business is to sit still, for I know best what is to be done. Do you act, now you are pilot, in the same manner: I, as it becomes a passenger, will sit quiet and obey.

MERCURY.

You are right. I know very well what is to be done, and will look out a proper place. Let me see—what do you think of Caucasus? or Parnassus still higher? or Olympus higher than both? Stay—while I am staring at Olympus, a thought is come into my head—but I shall want your help.

CHARON.

CHARON.

Only say the word: I will do my very best.

MERCURY.

Homer the poet tells us, that the [c] two sons of Aloeus, when they were but lads, took it into their heads, that, by tearing Ossa up by the roots, and piling it upon Olympus, with Pelion between, they might furnish out a very convenient ladder, to climb up to Heaven by. The young rascals were deservedly punished for their impudence. But I see no manner of reason why we two may not follow their manner of building, and roll mountains upon mountains; since we have no ill designs against the gods, and only intend mending our prospect.

CHARON.

You do not suppose that we two have strength to lift up Pelion or Ossa!

MERCURY.

No! what, do you think that we two gods cannot match a couple of snivelling infants?

[c] Hom. Odyſ. ii. ver. 311.

CHARON.

CHARON.

Yes; but it is a difficult task, let me tell you.

MERCURY.

You are an illiterate fellow, Charon, not conversant in poetry. The good man Homer has the knack of compounding mountains so readily, that, at the expence of only two lines, he makes you a high road to heaven. But I wonder you should think this any thing extraordinary, when you cannot but know how Atlas bears up the world, which bears up you and me and all of us. Did you never hear, that my brother Hercules gave him a little respite, putting his own back under the burden?

CHARON.

I have heard such stories undoubtedly: but how true they are, you and the poets may look to that.

MERCURY.

True! they are most certainly true. What, do you think, should make such wise men lie? So let us fairly fall to work, and weigh up Ossa first,

first, as our Architect's poem prescribes. Then Pelion all [d] trembling with tears will we set upon Ossa. Only mind how easily and poetically we have done the business! I will get up, and see if it be high enough, or whether we must lay on more. Alas! we have hardly got to the skirts of Heaven! One can but just discern Ionia and Lydia on the East, and Italy and Sicily on the west. On the north one may just make out the parts about the Ister, and that way is a dim appearance of Crete. We must go to work again, Mr. Ferryman, and hoist up Oeta too, and then set Parnassus on the top of all.

CHARON.

Yes, but let us take care of making our work too flight; left, if we do, we should break our necks from our Homerical edifice.

MERCURY.

Never fear: all will be safe enough. First remove Oeta; and then let us have Parnassus. Now I will make a second experiment. O rare! I can see every thing. Come, come, get up.

[d] Επιπιτυλλει.

CHARON.

CHARON.

Pr'ythee, Mercury, lend me a hand: it is not so very easy to get up such a height.

MERCURY.

You want to see every thing, Charon: there is no such thing as gratifying your curiosity without some risque of a fall. But lay hold of my hand, and mind where you set your foot. Well done! now you are up. Parnassus, you see, has two tops; so let each of us take one for a seat. Now look all round you, and observe.

CHARON.

I see much land, with a vast lake surrounding it. I see also mountains, and rivers larger than Cocytus and Periphlegethon. Then there are little things of men too, and their caves.

MERCURY.

Caves! those caves, as you call them, are cities.

CHARON.

Do you know, Mercury, that we have been yet doing nothing at all? We might as well have

have left Parnassus at rest with its fountain, and never disturbed Oeta and these other huge hills.

MERCURY.

Why so?

CHARON.

There is no perceiving any thing with exactness from such a height. I did not only want to see mountains and cities, as one sees them in a map; but to see the men, to hear what they say, and see what they do. Just as when we two met, you found me laughing, and asked me the reason; I had just heard something, which delighted me extremely.

MERCURY.

What was it?

CHARON.

A man had promised his friend to sup with him the next day; and before the words were well out of his mouth, a tile (Heaven knows who threw it) fell from the house-top, and beat his brains out. I laughed at his not keeping his word.—But there is no seeing or hearing any thing well here: I shall go down.

MERCURY.

MERCURY.

Be quiet: I will remedy the inconvenience you complain of, and cure your shortsightedness in an instant, by the application of only a scrap of Homer. But remember to make a proper use of the charm: you must blunder no more.

CHARON.
Well, what is it?

MERCURY.
[r] The cloud, which veil'd thy eyes, I took away,
That gods and men might seem in open day.

CHARON.
Humph!

MERCURY.
Now can you see?

CHARON.
See! Lynceus [f] himself never saw half so clearly! Now, I hope, you will give me information in answer to my enquiries. Simple

[r] Hom. Il. v. ver. 127.
[f] Who could see distinctly 130 miles, or thereabouts.

as I sit here, I also know something of Homer: will you let me ask questions from him?

MERCURY.

How should an old Ferryman, who is continually tugging his oars, know any thing of Homer?

CHARON.

Do not upbraid me with my profession. I carried him over, after he died, and still remember something of the many songs, which he favoured us with. You must know we had an exceeding bad passage. For Homer having begun a ditty inauspicious to the passengers, about Neptune's collecting the clouds, and raising a commotion in the waves, by striking his trident into the sea, like a ladle into a porridge-pot; how he raised all the storms, and tumbled about the waters—while he was thus confounding the sea with his verses, on a sudden, such a tempest, with so black a cloud, fell upon us, that it was a hundred to one our vessel was not turned topsy-turvy. Homer himself was seasick,

CHARON. 83

sick, and [g] vomited up a great deal of his poem, with Scylla, Charybdis, and Cyclops.

MERCURY.

It was no hard matter then for you to pick up a little from so copious a discharge.

CHARON.

But tell me,
[h] What mighty fellow's that, so big, so tall,
By head and shoulders overtopping all?

MERCURY.

That is Milo, the wrestler of Croton, famous amongst the Greeks, for carrying a bull on his back over the Olympick race-ground.

CHARON.

I think I am a much greater man, who must soon take up Milo himself, and put him aboard

---

[g] It was the pride of ancient bards to see themselves represented in the same picture with Homer; in which they were employed in swallowing greedily and thankfully whatever evacuation their father vouchsafed to make. Γαλατῶν δ ζωγραφος εγραψε τον μεν Ὁμηρον αυτον εμουντα, τους δε αλλους ποιητας τα εμημεσμενα αρυομενους. Ælian. V. H. xiii. 22.

[h] Hom. Il. iii. ver. 226.

of my little boat. Death, that invincible champion, will give him a fall in a way unknown to him; after which he will lament not a little, when he thinks of his former honours. At present my gentleman is proud enough of being so much admired for carrying the bull. I wonder whether he has any notion of dying.

MERCURY.

Would you have him think of dying, in the very prime of life?

CHARON.

Let him alone. It will not be long before he will afford us excellent sport, in his passage over the Styx. He, who can now carry a bull, will not then have strength to lift a gnat.— But who is that other grave venerable gentleman? He is no Greek, by his dress.

MERCURY.

That man, Charon, is Cyrus, the son of Cambyses, who transferred the empire of the Medes to the Persians. Since that he has overcome the Assyrians, and subdued Babylon. He is now preparing an expedition into Lydia;

that,

that, having conquered Crœsus, he may be king over all.

CHARON.

And where is that Crœsus?

MERCURY.

Look that way to that great castle, fortified by a triple wall; that is Sardis. Do not you see Crœsus there, sitting on a golden throne, conferring with Solon the Athenian? shall we listen to what they say?

CHARON.

By all means.

CRŒSUS.

And now, my Athenian friend, you have seen my riches, beheld my immense treasures, the abundance of my bullion, the furniture of my palace, equally elegant and expensive: tell me, who, in your opinion, is the happiest man?

CHARON.

What do you think Solon will say?

MERCURY.

MERCURY.

Depend upon it, Charon, he will say something to the purpose.

SOLON.

Few, very few, O Crœsus, can be called happy; but, of all my acquaintance, I think that Cleobis and Biton, sons of the Priestess, are most so.

CHARON.

He means the sons of the Argive Priestess: they died together, after having drawn their mother in a waggon to the Temple.

CRŒSUS.

Well, they are happiest! and pray who is next to them?

SOLON.

Tellus, the Athenian, who, after living a life of virtue, died for his country.

CRŒSUS.

But do not you think, you poor rascal, that I am happy?

SOLON.

SOLON.

There is no judging, Crœsus, as yet; because you have not run your race. The hand of death points out the degree of happiness: a happy life must be a life well ended.

CHARON.

Well said, Solon! you are much in the right. It is my boat, which brings things to a crisis.—But who are those fellows that Crœsus is dispatching, and what are those loads on their backs?

MERCURY.

He is going to dedicate ingots of gold to Apollo, in return for an oracle, which will be the [i] ruin of him. The poor man is wonderfully fond of fortune-tellers.

CHARON.

[i] Crœsus sending to the Oracle at Delphi to know the issue of his war, and continuance of his kingdome, was answered to the first, that if he made war with the Persians, he should overthrow a great kingdome; and to the second, that his estate should suffer no alteration till such time as a mule should raigne over the Medes: thus he making construction of the former, the best way for himself, and grounding upon the impossibilitie of the later, brought his kingdome

CHARON.

Is that gold, that shining [k] pale red thing? This is the very first time I ever saw that which I have heard so much about.

MERCURY.

That is the name: it is that celebrated thing, for which the world is in arms.

CHARON.

I can see nothing it is good for, unless it be to overload those who carry it.

---

dome to destruction, and himself to ruine; but afterwards questioning Apollo for the truth of the Oracle, was answered that the Oracle was not in the fault, but his owne misconstruction, for by the great kingdom was not meant the Persians but his owne, and that of the mule was made good in Cyrus his conquerour, who was borne of parents of divers countries, his mother being daughter to Astyages king of the Medes, and his father a Persian and a subject, and was so in all things like a mule which is begotten by a hee asse and a mare, being more noble by the mother's side than the father's. Francis Hicks. Herodotus.

[k] The Antients constantly attribute some degree of paleness to gold. Diogenes, being asked the reason why gold looked pale, said, it was owing to fear. Diogenes Laertius, VI. 51.

MERCURY.

CHARON.

MERCURY.

Little do you know how many wars, plots, robberies, perjuries, murders, prisons, what long voyages, what traffick, what slavery—

CHARON.

To get gold! O heaven and earth! which is something better than brass! I can speak to this point, because I am well acquainted with brass, exacting a piece of every passenger.

MERCURY.

True. But brass is not valued, because it is so plentiful. But, to obtain a bit of the other precious thing, men are glad to dig out the bowels of the earth. It is born of the same parents, you observe, as lead and other metals.

CHARON.

How stupid are mankind, to be thus besotted!

MERCURY.

Solon does not appear to be greatly in love with it. He is laughing at Crœsus, and despising his barbarous pride. He questions him about somewhat. Let us listen.

SOLON.

SOLON.

Do you suppose, Crœsus, that Apollo has any want of these ingots?

CRŒSUS.

Want! by Jupiter, all Delphi cannot produce such an offering!

SOLON.

And you think to make a happy God of him, by adding to his possessions these ingots of gold!

CRŒSUS.

Yes.

SOLON.

There must be very poor doings in Heaven, if, when the gods want gold, they must fetch it from Lydia.

CRŒSUS.

In what other place could such plenty be had?

SOLON.

Does Lydia produce iron?

CRŒSUS.

CRŒSUS.

No.

SOLON.

Then you want the better metal.

CRŒSUS.

What! iron better than gold!

SOLON.

If you will only keep your temper, and answer my queſtions, I can make it appear.

CRŒSUS.

Speak then.

SOLON.

Who merit the greater praiſe, the defenders, or the defended?

CRŒSUS.

The defenders aſſuredly.

SOLON.

Well then, if Cyrus ſhould make an inroad into Lydia, (and they ſay he deſigns it) would you give golden ſwords to your men? or would not iron ones be more commodious?

CRŒSUS.

CRŒSUS.

Iron would be better.

SOLON.

And, if iron is not provided, that immense heap of gold of yours must fall into the hands of the Persians.

CRŒSUS.

Softly, my good friend; have a care what you say.

SOLON.

Nay, I wish not for such an event. But you plainly see by the supposition, that iron is to be preferred.

CRŒSUS.

Then, I suppose, you would have me countermand my golden ingots, and make Apollo an offering of iron?

SOLON.

I fancy the God has as little occasion for the one as the other. But, whether you consecrate brass, or gold, or whatever you will, it will be only setting so much apart for others, for Phocis,

Phocis, for Bœotia, or Delphi, for some king, or some robber. As to Apollo, I promise you, he cares not a rush for goldmongers.

CRŒSUS.

You are for ever quarrelling and grumbling about my riches.

MERCURY.

You see, Charon, that the Lydian can bear any thing better than the plain truth. He thinks it a thing unaccountable, that a poor man should speak his mind to him without trembling. But he will find occasion to remember Solon by and by, when, being made prisoner by Cyrus, he shall be obliged to ascend the burning pile. I lately overheard Clotho reading the book of fate, in which every man's destiny is set down; and, amongst other things, it was decreed, that Crœsus should be taken prisoner by Cyrus, and that Cyrus himself should be slain by a woman. Do you see that Scythian queen there, riding upon a white horse?

CHARON.

Yes.

MERCURY.

MERCURY.

That is Tomyris, who is to cut off Cyrus's head, and throw it into a veſſel full of blood. Do you ſee that youth, the ſon of Cyrus? That is Cambyſes, who is to ſucceed his father in the empire; and who, after a thouſand blunders in Libya and Æthiopia, ſhall kill Apis [*l*]; and die mad.

CHARON.

Ridiculous! at preſent there is no ſuch thing as looking them in the face, they are ſo proud forſooth. Indeed who could believe, that one of them will ſoon be a priſoner, and the other have his inſatiable throat drenched in blood?—But who is that, Mercury, buttoned up in a purple robe, with a diadem on his head, to whom

In circled iſle, the cook preſents a ring,
Cut from a fiſh; who boaſts himſelf a king [*m*]?

[*l*] Apis was a king of Ægypt, who underſtood Huſbandry; for which reaſon, he was, after his death, worſhipped as an ox. The Iſraelites, who could not entirely conquer their Ægyptian prejudice, adored a calf.

[*m*] Hom. Od. I. ver. 50 and 180.

MERCURY.

MERCURY.

O rare Charon! you can say, and sing too! That is Polycrates [*n*], the tyrant of Samos, who plumes himself on being completely happy. He shall be betrayed by Mæandrius, his domestick who stands by him, into the hands of Orætes, who will hang him on a gibbet, parting him and his happiness in a moment. This too I heard from Clotho.

CHARON.

Bravely done, Clotho! Go on, cut off their heads, and crucify them, till they begin to think they are but men. Exalt them highly, that they may fall heavily. I shall laugh to see every man of them stark naked in my boat.

[*n*] Polycrates, after an uninterrupted flow of prosperity, was advised by Amasis king of Ægypt, to keep fortune in her present humour, by giving her that which he valued most. Accordingly he threw into the sea with great form his favourite ring. But, after a few days, a fine fish being presented to him, which was thought too good for any body else, the ring was found in its belly. This being considered as portending no good to Polycrates, the prudent Amasis would have nothing more to do with him. It was better, he thought, to desert a friend, than to feel his distress. Herodotus, p. 112. Cicero de finibus, near the end.

No purple, no tiara, no golden beds are there!

MERCURY.

Such is human greatness!—But do not you see a vast multitude of people, sailors, soldiers, lawyers, farmers, usurers, beggars?

CHARON.

I see a motley multitude truly, and the world full of confusion; cities like swarms of bees, in which every one has a sting to destroy his neighbour. Those, who cannot defend themselves, are ransacked, robbed, and pillaged by the wasps [o].—But that obscure troop which hovers about, who are they?

MERCURY.

Those, Charon, are Hope, and Fear, and Folly, and Pleasure, and Avarice, and Anger, and Hatred, and Jealousy, and Doubt. Fear and Hope fly over head: the former strikes, per-

---

[o] Ουγχι δε τινας ωσπερ σφηκας, αγουσι και φερουσι τον ντωδοτερον. It is wonderful that so many learned men should render this αγουσι και φερουσι agunt feruntque. See Pearce's Longinus, p. 173.

plexes, and confounds: the latter, but juſt out of reach, when men moſt think of ſeizing it, on a ſudden gives them the ſlip, and leaves the fools gaping after it; juſt as you have ſeen Tantalus ſerved by the water, conſtantly eluding his thirſty lips. If you obſerve, you will ſee the Parcæ ſpinning out human deſtiny; every man is fixed to a ſpindle, by threads as fine as a ſpider's web.

CHARON.

I ſee a very ſlender ſtring that every man muſt hold by; which is generally interwoven and entangled with ſome other.

MERCURY.

Even ſo, Mr. Waterman. For it is decreed that one man ſhall be killed by another, and that other by a third; this man ſhall be heir to one with a ſhorter thread, and another to him. This explains the connexion you obſerve amongſt the ſeveral threads. How weak is the line that every one hangs by! This man is ſeen very high, ſuſpended aloft: but the thread will break with his weight, and the fall will be the greater. Another, who was raiſed but a little, falls

falls with little noise, and is hardly taken notice of by his neighbours.

CHARON.

Truly, Mercury, you give a pleasant account of mankind!

MERCURY.

No words can sufficiently express their folly. Whilst full of hope, and emulous in absurdity, comes arbiter Death, and ends the dispute! Death, you see, employs many messengers and agents, as agues, fevers, consumptions, peripneumonies, swords, thieves, poison, judges, tyrants. Alackaday! while the world wags well, they never once think of any of these. But, if once their matters miscarry, immediately all is weeping and wailing. Surely, if they would set out with the resolution to believe themselves mortal, and that they are to sojourn but a short space in this world, and then to depart, as out of a dream;—if they would but consider the necessity of leaving every thing behind them, they could not but live more wisely, and die with less concern. As it is, they act as if their
enjoyments

enjoyments on earth were to laſt for ever.
When therefore the miniſter of Death calls them
aſide, and carries them away fettered by a fever
or confumption, they are pleaſed to take it extremely ill, and be very angry; they do not
underſtand ſuch uſage, and never dreamed of
being dragged away in this manner. A man
would ſcarcely be in ſuch a hurry of building,
if he knew he was haſtening to his own end,
and that before he ſaw the roof well laid, he
muſt give up the houſe to his heir, without ever
eating or drinking in it. The father of a newborn ſon, who entertains his friends ſo chearfully, and is ſo pleaſed with communicating
his own name, would not be ſo much elevated
with joy, if he knew that his boy is to die at
the age of ſeven years. The cauſe of his rejoicing is, that he thinks of nothing but the happy father, whoſe ſon is diſtinguiſhed by fame,
victorious at the Olympick games. Alas! he
regards not his neighbour, who is bearing his
child to the funeral pile, nor bethinks himſelf
how ſlenderly he was ſuſpended. What wrangling and contending you ſee about the limits
of a hedge! what an endleſs raking and ſcraping

ing together of money! but, before the day of enjoyment, behold the arrival of those messengers of Fate!

CHARON.

I see how matters go; and am thinking with myself, what there can be so very engaging in life, that makes men so unwilling to leave it.

MERCURY.

If any one should examine the condition of kings, who seem to be the happiest of all men, and beyond the reach of uncertainty and ill fortune; he would find their sorrows much more numerous than their joys: to such fears, confusion, hatred, plotting, rage, and flattery, are the wretched things called princes exposed! I mention not the sorrows, diseases, and distresses, which are equally incident to men of all conditions. And, if such be the condition of a king, it is not difficult to imagine that of a private man.

CHARON.

I will tell you, Mercury, what I have been thinking of. You have seen the bubbles, that
compose

compose the froth, in a rapid fall of water; of which some are small, and burst almost as soon as formed; some last longer, and, being united with others, swell to a considerable size; yet these too soon disappear: such is human life. All men are puffed up with air, some more, some less. Some can just for a moment keep up the inflation; others lose it before they well have it; but all, like bubbles, must burst at last.

MERCURY.

Your simile, in my mind, is not inferior to that of Homer, who compares the generations of men to the [*p*] leaves of trees.

CHARON.

Yet, such as they are, you see, Mercury, how they behave! how they quarrel about dignities, honours, and possessions! all which they will be obliged to leave behind them, except one poor obolus for me! I have a good mind (now we are upon an eminence) to call out as loud as I can, advising them to forbear their idle

[*p*] Hom. Il. vi. ver. 146.

pursuits, and live, as they ought to do, in daily expectation of death.—Holla! have done, ye fools! What would ye be at? You are not to stay in this world for ever! not one of these fine things will last! there is no taking them with you, when you die! you must quit the premises stark naked! houses and land and money must perpetually be changing their masters!— Do not you think, Mercury, that, if I were to bawl all this truth in their ears, they would turn over a new leaf, and mend their manners?

MERCURY.

O Charon, how you talk! They are so choaked up with ignorance and error, that you could not open their ears with an auger. Ulysses [q] did not more effectually guard his companions against the songs of the Syrens, by filling their ears with wax. You might roar till you split; it would be all in vain; for ignorance operates to the same effect here, as the potion of Lethe below. And yet it must be owned there are a few attentive to the voice of truth, and able to see and distinguish things as they really are.

[q] Hom. Od. xii. ver. 173.

CHARON.

CHARON.

Suppose then I should direct my admonition to them?

MERCURY.

That would be only to tell them what they already know. You see they are a people distinct from the rest, who heartily despise the things of this world, and are preparing to shew a fair pair of heels, and leave it. And indeed the world will forgive them when they do; for whoever reproves folly is sure to be hated for his pains.

CHARON.

Well done! brave fellows! though they are but few.

MERCURY.

It is well there are any.—But now let us go down.

CHARON.

There is yet one thing more which I would fain know; after which I cannot desire to give you any more trouble: where are the reposi-
tories,

tories, which they make in the earth, for dead bodies?

MERCURY.

You mean the graves, tombs, and sepulchres. Observe those hillocks, pillars, and pyramids [r] before the cities: all those are places, where dead bodies are received and laid up.

CHARON.

What do they mean by perfuming and placing garlands on the stones? There are some, who have raised up a pile before the heaps of earth, and have dug a pit, where they are burning expensive banquets. They pour wine into the hole, as far as I can see, together with a mixture of wine and water and honey.

MERCURY.

Really, Charon, I cannot see what good all this can do to persons in the other world. But

---

[r] The Ancients were not fond of poisoning their most frequented places with the effluvia of dead bodies. Only such as had greatly distinguished themselves in the publick service, were permitted to be buried within their cities, and especially in their temples. The Moderns are not so scrupulous in this particular.

they

they are persuaded, no doubt, that ghosts frequently take a turn up stairs, fluttering about the smoke of their graves, picking a bit of supper, or taking a little drink from the pit, as they can get it.

CHARON.

I should be a fool to suppose, that you, Mercury, who conduct them to me every day, should want to be informed, that those, whose skulls are as dry as dust, can neither eat nor drink. You can give a pretty good guess, whether a man, who is once fairly under ground, ever comes up again. I should be finely employed, if, besides my continual trouble to get them down, I must be obliged to bring them up again, to drink! O miserable fools! not to know the immense distance between the living and the dead, and how matters go amongst us!

> Buried, unburied, with, without a name,
> Iris and Agamemnon are the same!
> The head of Thetis' son, so fam'd, so fair,
> As ugly as Thersites' and as bare!
> Together in the daffodils they go,
> All dry, all naked, all alike below [1]!

[1] A Cento from Hom. Il. i. Od. 10. &c. A sly rogue, who loves to entrap unwary vanity, pretended to suspect, that these verses were stolen from Pope.

MERCURY.

MERCURY.

Bless me! you have all Homer by heart. But now you have just put it into my head, I can shew you the tomb of Achilles. There it is, on the promontory of Sigæum, near the sea. Over-against him in Rhœteum lies Ajax.

CHARON.

There is nothing grand in their monuments. But cannot you favour me with a sight of those famous cities, of which we have heard so much below? I mean Ninive, the city of Sardanapalus, Babylon, Mycenæ, Cleonæ, and Troy itself: from the town of Troy, for ten long years together, I well remember never to have had a moment's rest, being constantly employed in carrying over transports; nor could I once get my boat into dock, to refit.

MERCURY.

Ninive is so entirely destroyed, that you could not possibly find out the place where it stood. The great Babylon, which you see there, adorned with so many towers, and surrounded with
such

such a wall, in a little time will be no more to be found than Ninive is at present. I am ashamed to shew you Mycenæ, and Cleonæ; but especially Troy. It would be enough to make you take Homer by the collar at your return home; in such pompous terms has he described it, These cities had their day, which now is over. Whole towns, Mr. Waterman, die like men; and, what is more wonderful, rivers too. Inachus, the famed flood of Argi, has now no remains.

CHARON.

How idle were all the praises, how vain the extravagant epithets of Homer! the sacred Ilion! the beautiful Cleonæ! alas! alas!—But, whilst we are talking, who are they that are fighting and killing one another yonder? what is it for?

MERCURY.

They are the Argives and Lacedæmonians. Othryades [1], the general of the latter, scarcely alive, is inscribing a trophy with his blood.

CHARON.

[1] Three hundred Lacedæmonians and as many Argives were deputed to fight for the plain of Thyria; of all which
only

CHARON.

But what do they fight for?

MERCURY.

For the field they fight in.

CHARON.

Oh! what palpable abſurdity! Are they ignorant, that, though every man of them had as much as all Peloponneſus, yet Æacus would hardly allow them a ſquare foot for their whole eſtate? The field will fall into many hands one after another, and his trophy will be often turned up by the plough.

MERCURY.

So indeed it will be. But let us go down, and leave the mountains where we found them; that we may go about our buſineſs, you to your ſculler, and I on my errand. It ſhall not be a great while before I bring you ſome ghoſts.

only three ſurvived the battle. Alcinor and Cromius returned to Argi, as they ſuppoſed, victorious. While their enemy Othryades, remaining in the field, plundered their countrymen, and wrote his triumphant name on his ſhield with his own blood.

CHARON.

CHARON.

I am so much obliged to you, Mercury, that I can never forget the service you have done me on this occasion as long as I live.—Alas! alas! how miserable mortals spend their time!—kings!—golden ingots!—hecatombs!—battles!——but not a syllable about Charon!

THE

THE
INFERNAL PASSAGE:
OR,
THE TYRANT.

On the Vices of KINGS.

THE INFERNAL PASSAGE:
OR,
THE TYRANT[a].

CHARON.

ALL is ready, Clotho. The boat has been prepared this good while, and is in excellent condition. I have pumped out the water, set up the mast, spread the sail, and bound fast the oars in their places; and nothing is wanting on my part to prevent us weighing

---

[a] The Tyrrheni were a mischievous people, very troublesome to the Athenians. From their name, it is pretended, was derived the word *tyrant*, which was however in better repute than its original, being, for some time, synonymous with *king*.

anchor,

anchor, and failing immediately. Only Mercury is not come, who ought to have been here long ago. You see I have not a single passenger. If he had supplied me as he ought, I might have made three trips this very day already. And, now it is almost night, I have not earned a single obolus. I know very well Pluto will blame me for this delay, though I am as innocent as the child unborn. He is a fine purveyor of ghosts! I fancy he has met with a cup of Lethe above, and has forgot his way back again. Perhaps my gentleman is wrestling with the youngsters, or twanging his harp, or telling long stories, to prove his skill in trifling. Or perhaps the honest fellow is employed in thieving by the way: for that too is one of his accomplishments. We have a full right to one half of his time and attention; and, I cannot but say, he takes a good deal of liberty with us.

CLOTHO.

How do you know, Charon, that he is not detained by some extraordinary business of Jupiter? Jupiter is master, and will be obeyed.

CHARON.

CHARON.

Yes; but why should he keep him beyond his time? I am sure we have never detained him with us, when it was his duty to be gone. But I believe I can guess the cause. With us there is nothing but daffodil, and libations, and cakes, and obsequies, in mists, and clouds, and darkness; but in Heaven all is splendid and gay, ambrosia abounds, and nectar goes jovially round. No wonder therefore my gentleman likes to be there. When he leaves us, he flies like a thief from a gaol. But, when he is to return, he does it indeed at last, but it is with great deliberation and reluctance.

CLOTHO.

Hold your tongue, Charon! for here he comes! Do not you see him with his rod driving a whole swarm before him, like a flock of goats? what can be the meaning of this? One of them is chained, another ready to split with laughing, a third with a wallet and a cudgel, looking plaguily four, and pushing on the rest. As to Mercury himself, he is all over in a sweat, puffing and blowing for breath, with his feet covered

covered with duft. What is the matter, Mercury? why such hurry and flutter?

MERCURY.

Matter? matter enough! I have had such a piece of work with pursuing this run-away rascal, that I verily thought I should not have reached the boat to-day.

CLOTHO.

But who is he? and what could he mean by attempting an escape?

MERCURY.

The reason of that is plain enough: he wanted to live a while longer, to be sure. I guess him to be some king, some tyrant; such a howling he has made, and so bitterly has he bewailed the loss of his enjoyments.

CLOTHO.

What! when his thread was spun to the end, did the fool think of running away from inevitable fate?

MERCURY.

Think of running away! do you say? I tell you, that, if my honest friend here with the
staff

staff had not helped me to lay hold of him and bind him, he would have got from us, as sure as you are there. From his being first delivered up to me by Atropos, he constantly hung behind, he pitched his feet against the ground, and was so refractory, that it was with the utmost difficulty I could get him along. Sometimes he tried gentle means; he begged and prayed of me only to let him go for a moment, for which he promised an ample reward. Knowing that the man made a request which could not possibly be granted, you may be sure I paid no regard to it. But, when we were got to the very entrance, and I, as usual, was reckoning up my dead to Æacus [w], and he was comparing my account with the tally sent him by your sister, I know not how it was, that this abominable villain sneaked away and got off, leaving me one short of my number. Upon this, Æacus, knitting his brows, said, he would have none of my tricks here; I might be contented with playing the rogue in Heaven.

[w] Lucian here seems to have forgot himself a little. According to all the geographers, Æacus lived on the other side of the river. Moses du Soul.

"There is no place here, says he, for subterfuge of any kind: whatever relates to the dead must be exact. According to this tally, you should have brought a thousand and four; unless you pretend that Atropos has imposed upon you." I was greatly confounded by what he said, and presently called to mind what had passed by the way. When, looking all round and not seeing the fellow, I soon concluded that he had given me the slip. Upon which, taking the direct road back to day-light, I ran as fast as my feet could carry me; while this worthy gentleman very civilly accompanied me. We ran like two racers, and came up with him in [*] Tænaros; so very near was he to making his escape.

CLOTHO.

And we, Charon, had been all this while blaming Mercury for his idleness!

CHARON.

Well, but why should we stay here now? We have been delayed long enough already.

[*] A promontory of Laconia, from whence was supposed to be a passage to the other world. Πυλη τις ετι Ταιναρου ωρος ωχροη. Menand. fragm.

CLOTHO.

CLOTHO.

Right; let them go aboard. I will sit down by the ladder, and, with the catalogue in my hand, as my custom is, will inform myself concerning them all separately as they enter, who they are, whence they come, and in what manner they died. Do you, Mercury, take and stow them properly. The new-born infants you may throw in first, as they can give no account of themselves.

MERCURY.

Here are three hundred of them for you, Mr. Ferryman, including foundlings.

CHARON.

A fine prize! You gather the fruit before it is ripe.

MERCURY.

Next to them, Clotho, would you have me put aboard those who died unlamented?

CLOTHO.

You mean the old: do so. Why should I trouble myself with enquiring into what was done before Euclid [*y*]? All ye, who are upwards of threescore, make your appearance! Holla!—They are so deaf with age, I find, they cannot hear. Perhaps it will be necessary to hoist them on board.

MERCURY.

Well, here are three hundred and ninety-eight, all ripe and mellow, not reaped before the harvest.

CLOTHO.

No truly; these are dry grapes. Now, Mercury, bring up the wounded. Tell me first of all how ye came by your death: or, stay; I can recognize you by the respective decrees concerning you. Eighty-four were yesterday to die fighting in Media, and, amongst these, Gobares the son of Oxyartes.

MERCURY.

Here they are.

[*y*] After the expulsion of the thirty tyrants by Thrasybulus, the Athenians, for the sake of peace, had passed an act of oblivion, respecting every transaction before the government of Euclid.

CLOTHO,

CLOTHO.

Seven despairing lovers dispatched themselves. Theagenes, the philosopher, left the world for a Megarensian harlot.

MERCURY.

They are all here.

CLOTHO.

And where are they who butchered one another for the sake of empire?

MERCURY.

Here.

CLOTHO.

And the man slain by his wife and her gallant?

MERCURY.

Here, before you.

CLOTHO.

Bring up those who died by due course of law, by tortures and the gallows, and the sixteen murdered by highway-men.

MERCURY.

MERCURY.

Here you have them, mangled as they are.—
Would you have me bring up the women too?

CLOTHO.

Yes; and those who perished together in shipwreck, and then those who died of the fever. And do not forget the Doctor Agathocles: put him with his patients.—But where is Cyniscus, the philosopher? He was to die after eating the supper of Hecate, expiation-eggs, and raw cuttle-fish.

CYNISCUS.

I am here, Clotho, at your service. I beg to know for what offence you suffered me to remain so long upon earth? My spindle was almost full. Very glad should I have been to come sooner, and often wished to snap my thread; but somehow or other I found it impracticable.

CLOTHO.

I left you as the inspector and physician of human failings;—but now go aboard and welcome!

CYNISCUS.

CYNISCUS.

I cannot go till this prisoner is put into the boat: he has so insinuating a tongue, that I am afraid he will warp you from your purpose.

CLOTHO.

Let me see who he is.

MERCURY.

Megapenthes the tyrant, the son of Lacydes.

CLOTHO.

Go aboard, Megapenthes.

MEGAPENTHES.

No, pray, good Madam, let me go back only for a little while. I will come again, sweet Clotho, upon my word, without being sent for, or giving any more trouble.

CLOTHO.

What is it that makes you so very desirous of going back?

MEGAPENTHES.

I beg only to finish a house I was building, I only beg —

CLOTHO.

CLOTHO.

The man raves! Get in, make haste.

MEGAPENTHES.

I am not unreasonable, O Destiny; I only beg to stay one single day, just to give my wife directions about my estate, and shew her where my great treasure is buried.

CLOTHO.

You may make yourself easy: it cannot be.

MEGAPENTHES.

What, must all that money be lost then?

CLOTHO.

No, not lost; be satisfied about that; your cousin Megacles will have it.

MEGAPENTHES.

Oh scandalous! what, my enemy? I spared his life only for want of leisure to kill him.

CLOTHO.

He is the man. He will survive you upwards of forty years, and be master of all your women, money, and clothes.

MEGA-

MEGAPENTHES.

This is very unfair in you, Clotho, to give a man's possessions to his greatest enemies.

CLOTHO.

Pray, good Sir, how came you by these possessions? were they not the property of Cydimachus? did not you murder him? and, before the breath was out of his body, did not you cut the throats of his children, before his face?

MEGAPENTHES.

Well, but what he had was mine now.

CLOTHO.

And now, Sir, your lease expires.—

MEGAPENTHES.

But I want to speak a word or two in private with you, Clotho: step this way a little. Hark you; if you will suffer me to make my escape, I promise to give you this very day a thousand talents [z] of gold coin.

[z] 193,750 pounds.

CLOTHO

CLOTHO.

Ridiculous puppy! have you not done thinking of your money yet?

MEGAPENTHES.

Besides, to oblige you, I will give you two cups, for which I murdered Cleocritus: either of them weighs a [a] hundred talents of the purest gold.

CLOTHO.

Seize this fellow here! he would never go by his own will.

MEGAPENTHES.

Consider, the city wall and the harbour for shipping remain both unfinished; which, if I had lived only five days longer, would have been done.

CLOTHO.

Never mind; another man will build.

[a] 5691 lb. 11 oz. 11 dwts. 10 gr.⁶⁄₇ or 41 cwt. 3 qrs. 12 lb. 1 oz. ₇⁴₆; the pound troy, according to Arbuthnot, being to the avoirdupois as 14 to 17.

MEGAPENTHES.

I have one request, which, I am sure, you must allow to be a reasonable one.

CLOTHO.

What is it?

MEGAPENTHES.

Only that I may live till I subdue the Pisidians, and make the Lydians tributary, and rear up a magnificent monument for myself, inscribing upon it all the great exploits of generalship which I have performed.

CLOTHO.

Heyday! it would require twenty years to do all this. One day indeed!

MEGAPENTHES.

Nay, I am ready to give bail for my speedy return. I will give up my favourite to you as a pledge for myself.

CLOTHO.

Oh the villain! how often have you prayed that he might survive you!

MEGA-

MEGAPENTHES.

Yes, when I knew no better.

CLOTHO.

He will be with you soon, for the new king will dispatch him.

MEGAPENTHES.

One thing at least, Clotho, you cannot refuse me.

CLOTHO.

What is that?

MEGAPENTHES.

Only to know what turn affairs will take after my death.

CLOTHO.

I will tell you; though it will only vex you the more. As to your wife, the slave Midas will have her—not that she will be any novelty to him.

MEGAPENTHES.

The accursed villain, whom I made free at her request!

CLOTHO.

CLOTHO.

Your daughter will add one more to the new king's concubines. The pictures and statues, which the city erected to your honour, are all thrown down, and every body laughs to see them.

MEGAPENTHES.

And do none of my friends resent such doings?

CLOTHO.

Friends? I know of none you had. How could you pretend to think of having friends? You surely must be sensible that all who adored you, and praised every thing you did and said, did it either out of fear, or for their own interest. Such friends are the friends of power, and cannot last.

MEGAPENTHES.

But at banquets, amidst libations of wine, how loudly did they pray for my everlasting prosperity! They swore by me, and, if it were but possible, were ready to die in my room.

CLOTHO.

CLOTHO.

You supped yesterday with one of those devoted friends; and the last cup, which he gave you, sent you a packing hither.

MEGAPENTHES.

I thought there was something bitter in the taste. But what could be his reason?

CLOTHO.

Come, get in. There is no end of your questions.

MEGAPENTHES.

One thing sticks very much in my stomach, which makes me long for a little day-light.

CLOTHO.

What important business is that?

MEGAPENTHES.

You must know that my man Carion, the moment he perceived that I was fairly dead, came in the evening into the room where I lay, and, finding the coast clear (for there was nobody to take care of me) he shut the door upon himself and Glycerium my concubine, and was as familiar with her in all respects as if no one else had been there. I suppose it was by no means the beginning of their acquaintance. When all was over, fixing his malicious eyes upon me, Rascal, says he, many a time have you beaten my poor bones for nothing. Saying that, he plucked me by the beard, and beat me on the face as hard as he could. At last he spat very copiously upon me, very civilly bade me go to hell, and took his leave. I was vexed to the heart; but what could I do? I was not in a capacity to be revenged on him. The wicked jade no sooner heard a noise of somebody coming, than, wetting her eyes with her spittle, she fell a weeping and lamenting most piteously, bewailing my death, and repeating my name as she went out—but if ever I catch them—

CLOTHO.

Have done with your threatening, and get aboard; it is high time for you to think of taking your trial.

MEGAPENTHES.

Who will presume to receive evidence against a king?

CLOTHO.

CLOTHO.

Nobody will againſt a king; but you will find one Rhadamanthus, who will take the liberty of judging and paſſing ſentence, with the greateſt regard to juſtice, on you and every other dead man. But come: you have delayed us already too long.

MEGAPENTHES.

Look you, Clotho, as to my being a king, I give up that point. Inſtead of a king, let me be a peaſant, or a ſlave, or any thing; only let me go back.

CLOTHO.

Where is our friend with the cudgel?—Mercury, you muſt drag this fellow into the boat neck and heels; there is no other way.

MERCURY.

Come along, you runaway ſcoundrel!—Take him, Charon, with that other; and, for ſecurity, let him be tied to the maſt.

MEGAPENTHES.

I hope at leaſt I am to have the firſt ſeat?

CLOTHO.

CLOTHO.

For what?

MEGAPENTHES.

For what? because I have been a king! because I have had ten thousand guards!

CLOTHO.

Carion might very well pluck the beard of such an insolent fellow! You shall taste of the sweets of royalty, administered to you by the cudgel.

MEGAPENTHES.

Cyniscus dare to lift up a stick against me! it is not so long ago, that I was within an ace of nailing the varlet to a post, for his insolence in my royal presence.

CHARON.

For which your majesty must be bound to the mast.—

MICYLLUS.

Pray, Clotho, is no notice at all to be taken of me? am I to be the very last to go aboard, because forsooth I am poor?

CLOTHO.

CLOTHO.

Who are you?

MICYLLUS.

I am Micyllus the cobler.

CLOTHO.

You are in a most prodigious hurry! here is a king, who would give I know not how much for a little respite. I wonder how it came to pass that you are so little disposed to stay.

MICYLLUS.

Good Clotho, hear what I have to say. I am not very highly delighted with the generosity of the [b] Cyclops, with the gracious promise of being devoured the last. Since, first or last, the same teeth will do the same office. Besides, my situation is totally different from that of the rich. The king, who seemed so happy, was so feared, and so admired; when he came to leave his gold, and silver, and fine clothes, and horses, and feasts, his fine women, and all his ministers of pleasure, could not but lament

[b] Hom. Od. ix. ver. 369.

lament most immoderately, and take it exceedingly unkind to be torn away from all that he held so dear. I know not how it is, but the soul of such a man sticks like birdlime to its dissolute habit, nor can they be separated without great difficulty. As if the chain, that binds them so closely, was not to be broken, whenever they are violently dragged away, they mourn and bewail their fate. Though bold enough on other occasions, no sooner do they set foot on this highway, than they become the veriest cowards in nature. Every now and then they must turn round, wishing, like unhappy lovers, for another look before they go; just as this fool here not only attempted an escape by the way, but must be begging and praying here. For my part, I had no engagements in the world, neither houses, nor land, nor gold, nor furniture, nor honour, nor images; so that I was always ready for a march: and the very moment that Atropos gave me the wink, I threw down my leather and paring-knife with pleasure, and ran away barefooted with the last in my hand, without staying to wash off the wax from my fingers. I ran even before my conductor, looking wishfully forwards. There was nothing behind that could tempt me to turn or look back. And upon my word, as far as I can judge, every thing with you is very fine. All are upon the same footing, no one presumes to lord it over his neighbour; which in truth is excellent. I do not imagine that there is any such thing here as paying of debts or taxes. And, what is best of all, there is no cold winter, no sickness to be dreaded, nor any being bemauled by our betters. All is peace and quietness. Indeed every thing is turned topsy-turvy: we, who are poor, laugh; while they, who are rich, lament.

CLOTHO.

I observe, Micyllus, you have been very merry this good while: pray what made you laugh so?

MICYLLUS.

O goddess most revered, I crave your patience. As I lived very near this king, I had an opportunity of being witness to his proceedings; and really I thought him as great as a God. Bless me! said I, when I saw his flowered ed purple, the multitude of his attendants, his gold, his goblets set with jewels, his bedsteads of silver! bless me! said I, how happy must he be! I was almost mad at the smell of his kitchen; I thought him more than man, and happy above the lot of human nature. Fairer, and taller, raised, by the grace of fortune, a royal cubit above others, he swelled as he walked, and, pompously unconcerned, put all he met out of countenance. But, when he was dead, and stripped of his prerogative, I thought him ridiculous enough. But I thought myself by far the greater fool of the two, for having so admired such a wretched animal, estimating his happiness by the fumes of his dishes, and his good fortune by the [c] blood of a Laronian cockle. However, he was not the only one who afforded me diversion. For, when I beheld Gniphon the usurer sighing, and repenting when it was too late, that he had cheated himself out of the enjoyment of all he had, which he must now leave entire to the abandoned Rhodochares, the heir at law—thinking of this,

[c] The purple-fish.

it was impossible to contain myself, when I recollected what a pale, wan, dirty, half-starved, wrinkled, pining, fretting, anxious, mortal he was. The only riches he possessed for use were his fingers, with which he [*d*] counted his talents and ten thousands, scraping together, by little and little, what the precious Rhodochares will scatter as fast.—But let us set sail, and laugh over what remains by the way, when we see the tears of our companions.

CLOTHO.

Get in, that Charon may weigh anchor.—

CHARON.

You, Sir! whither so fast? The boat is already full. — Stay till to-morrow morning, and I will give you a cast over.

MICYLLUS.

It is very hard, Charon, that I must be left behind, who am fairly dead, and well entitled to go. Depend upon it, you shall appear before Rhadamanthus for this. Alack! alack!

[*d*] His fingers served him as figures. See the note on Juvenal, Sat. x. ver. 249.

what an unlucky dog am I! now they fail, and I muſt be left alone! I will even jump in and ſwim: a dead man needs not be afraid of drowning. Beſides, if he would take me in, I have no money.

CLOTHO.

What now? Stay, Micyllus. You muſt not go over ſo.

MICYLLUS.

Very likely! I fancy I ſhall be over before you, for all that.

CLOTHO.

You cannot go ſo.—We muſt put to, and take him in. Lay hold of him, Mercury, lend him a hand.

CHARON.

And pray where is he to ſit? The boat is as full as it can be ſtowed.

MERCURY.

There is room for him upon the king's ſhoulders.

CLOTHO.

CLOTHO.

A good thought! get up immediately; do not spare the royal neck. A good voyage to us!

CYNISCUS.

It is best, Charon, to tell you the plain truth at once. I really have not an obolus to pay for my passage. This staff and this wallet are all that I have, believe me. But, if you would have me lend a hand at pumping or rowing, I am at your service. Give me but a good oar, and you shall see that I can use it.

CHARON.

Well, well, row then; and I shall be satisfied.

CYNISCUS.

Shall we have a cheer?

CHARON.

If you know a boatswain's [e] song, by all means let us have it.

[e] The tune probably was not unlike the recitative of our mariners when they hoist the sails.

CYNISCUS.

CYNISCUS.

Oh, yes. But behold! these fellows make such a howling, that nothing else can be heard.

A RICH MAN.

Alas! my possessions!

ANOTHER.

Alas! my estate!

ANOTHER.

Ah! woe is me! what a house have I left!

ANOTHER.

Oh! those talents of mine, which my prodigal heir will squander!

ANOTHER.

Alas! my poor infants!

ANOTHER.

Who will gather the grapes of my last year's vines?

MERCURY.

Why do not you weep, Micyllus? Nobody goes over without tears.

MICYL.

MICYLLUS.

Pish! I can find nothing to cry for, if we have but a good voyage.

MERCURY.

You must weep a little: it is the fashion.

MICYLLUS.

Well, to oblige you, Mercury, I will. Oh! my shoe-soles! oh! my old lasts! oh! my rotten shoes! oh! unhappy me! I shall no more sit fasting from morning to night! I must never more wander about, bare-footed, and in rags, my teeth chattering with cold! who shall inherit my paring-knife? who will enjoy my awl?—We have almost got over the water and my lamentation together.

CHARON.

Well, my masters, pay me my fare, before you leave me. You, Sir, where is your money? and your's? and your's, Sir? Every one has paid me except you, Micyllus. Come, come, do not trifle.

MICYL-

MICYLLUS.

It is yourself, Charon, who trifle moſt egregiouſly, if you expect any money from me. Whether an obolus be round or ſquare, is a matter quite unknown to Micyllus.

CHARON.

Upon my word, a good thriving voyage this! Get you gone. I muſt return to look after the horſes, oxen, dogs, and other animals, which are to come over.

CLOTHO.

Take theſe away, Mercury. I will ſail back to the oppoſite ſide, and bring with me Indopates and Heramithres, the Seres, who have knocked out one another's brains in a diſpute about a boundary.

MERCURY.

Come then, let us advance. Follow me in your turns; that is beſt.

MICYL.

MICYLLUS.

Oh! wonderful! what a mist here is! Where now is the handsome Megillus [*f*]? Phryne [*g*] is here no fairer than Simmiche [*g*]. All are alike, all of the same complexion; and, as for beauty, it is quite out of the question. Even my old greasy jacket is equally elegant with his majesty's purple; both of which are in the same obscurity.—But where are you, Cyniscus?

CYNISCUS.

Here, at your service. What, if you and I go on together?

MICYLLUS.

With all my heart: give me your hand. You have been initiated in the [*b*] mysteries of Eleusis: pray do the ceremonies there resemble the appearance of things here?

[*f*] A young Corinthian, remarkable for his fine person.

[*g*] Two Courtezans. Phryne carried on so lucrative a trade, that, after Thebes had been destroyed by Alexander the Great, it was rebuilt by Phryne the Greater.

[*b*] Certain rites solemnized in the night in honour of Ceres and Proserpine. See Warburton's dissertation on the sixth book of Virgil's Æneis.

CYNISCUS,

CYNISCUS.

Very much. But behold! what a frightful figure, shaking a torch, and looking most horribly sour! Is that one of the Furies?

MICYLLUS.

I fancy so, by her look.

MERCURY.

Here! Tisiphone, here are one thousand and four for you.

TISIPHONE.

Rhadamanthus has been waiting for you this good while.

RHADAMANTHUS.

Bring them up, Erinnys. Do you, Mercury, make proclamation, and call them over.

CYNISCUS.

I shall take it as a great favour, Rhadamanthus, if you will be pleased to let my examination come on first. I beg it for your [i] father's sake.

[i] Jupiter's.

RHADAMANTHUS.

Why?

CYNISCUS.

I want to give evidence against a certain person, whom I have known to be a sad rascal. And I would have it appear how I have behaved myself, before I accuse another; that my testimony may have the more weight.

RHADAMANTHUS.

And who are you?

CYNISCUS.

I am Cyniscus, my lord, by profession a philosopher.

RHADAMANTHUS.

Come then, take you your trial first.—Mercury, call his accusers.

MERCURY.

If any manner of person hath any thing to say against Cyniscus, let him come forth!

RHA-

RHADAMANTHUS.

Nobody appears! however, this is not sufficient. Strip yourself, Cyniscus, that I may see what [k] brands you have.

CYNISCUS.

How could I become branded?

RHADAMANTHUS.

As many sins as a man commits, so often, in a manner imperceptible, is he stigmatized in his soul.

CYNISCUS.

Examine me then; I am stripped, you see.

RHADAMANTHUS.

The man is quite free from any spots at all!—except that there are three or four little marks scarce distinguishable.—Yes, here are the scars. Pray how was this? how did you obliterate these brands, Cyniscus?

CYNISCUS.

I will tell you. Before I became a philosopher, I was guilty of many misdemeanors

[k] See Plato's Gorgias.

through ignorance, in confequence of which I contracted many ftains. But, applying myfelf to the ftudy of wifdom, by little and little I wafhed them out of my foul.

RHADAMANTHUS.

You certainly took the beft and moft effectual remedy.—As foon as you have given evidence againft the tyrant you mentioned, you may immediately repair to the [/] iflands of the bleffed, there to refide amongft people like yourfelf.—Call more.

MICYLLUS.

What relates to me may be very foon difpatched. I am already naked, Rhadamanthus, for your infpection.

RHADAMANTHUS.

Who are you?

MICYLLUS.

I am Micyllus, the cobler.

[/] Some have fancied thefe feats of blifs near the Straits of Gibraltar. Others have thought them fituated on the north of Scotland. It is but juftice to the fenfible fons of Caledonia to add, that they held no fuch abfurd opinion.

RHADAMANTHUS.

O rare Micyllus! There is no appearance of a spot in thee. Go with Cyniscus.—Now call the king.

MERCURY.

Megapenthes, the son of Lacydes, appear!—which way would you turn? Come up!—I call you, tyrant!—Take him by the collar, Tisiphone, and bring him up whether he will or no.—Now, Cyniscus, let us know, what you can lay to his charge: here he is.

CYNISCUS.

There is no great occasion for many words: it will appear from his brands what he is. However, to set the matter in the clearest light, I will endeavour to describe him and his behaviour. I shall pass over his enormities in private life. But, when, after associating with desperate fellows as wicked as himself, he raised guards, and advanced himself to sovereignty, he shewed his authority over the city by putting to death more than ten thousand persons, without any pretence whatever. By proceeding in this manner, and seizing on the effects of others,

he

he soon became immensely rich; and of course
stuck at nothing his libidinous heart could de-
vise. Every kind of cruelty, every species of
injury and insolence, his miserable subjects have
undergone! They were exposed to every extravagance of drunken riot: the innocence of neither sex escaped him. For his pride, his ar-
rogance, his haughty disdain of every one he
met, you can never sufficiently punish him. A
man might as safely confront the meridian sun,
as look with open eyes upon him. His un-
heard-of punishments, his genius for cruelty,
cannot be sufficiently set forth. Not even his
own family could escape his brutal rage. If
you suspect me of any prejudice against him,
you need only call the persons he has murdered, who will confirm what I say. And behold!
without being called, here they are! standing so
thick around him, that they are ready to stifle
him. All these, Rhadamanthus, have been murdered by this inhuman rascal. Some of them
were assassinated for having handsome wives;
others, because they could not bear his unnatural abuse of their children. To be rich, to be
wise, to be happy, to be virtuous enough to
dislike

INFERNAL PASSAGE.

dislike his abominable doings, was reason sufficient with him to put a man to death.

RHADAMANTHUS.

What do you answer, miscreant, to this charge? are you guilty, or not guilty?

MEGAPENTHES.

I own myself guilty of the murders. But I am innocent of the other crimes, the adulteries, the defiling of innocence, the unnatural debaucheries; concerning all which Cyniscus lies. He accuses me falsely.

CYNISCUS.

I am ready to make good my charge by undoubted evidence.

RHADAMANTHUS.

What witnesses will you call?

CYNISCUS.

Call hither, Mercury, his [m] lamp and his bed [n]: let them testify what they have been privy to.

MER.

[m] The introduction of such witnesses seems very repugnant to our ideas of propriety. But it might be intended,

MERCURY.

The bed and the lamp of Megapenthes, appear in court!—Very well, here they are.

RHADAMANTHUS.

Declare, each of you, what you know concerning this Megapenthes. And first let the Bed speak.

BED.

All is true that Cyniscus has accused him of. For my part, my Lord Rhadamanthus, I am ashamed to mention his practices on me.

RHADAMANTHUS.

Your testimony is sufficiently strong, since you cannot endure to recite his wickedness.— Now, Lamp, what have you to say?

LAMP.

I can say nothing to his behaviour by day, which, as I was not present, fell not under my observation. But I shudder to mention what passed in the night. I have seen numberless enormities not to be described, far surpassing all

as Bourdelotius thinks, to ridicule certain philosophers, who held that every thing had a soul. See Spectator, N° 56.

the rest; so that I often withheld my oil, and would have gladly withdrawn my light, which he applied to his most filthy purposes, and polluted all manner of ways.

RHADAMANTHUS.

There is no need of further evidence. Come, Sir, strip, off with your purple, that we may see how many scars you have. Astonishing! he is branded all over black and blue! no part of him but what is discoloured! What must we do with him? which way shall we punish him? shall he be tossed into Pyriphlegethon, or thrown to Cerberus?

CYNISCUS.

No. Give me leave to propose a new method of punishment not improper for him.

RHADAMANTHUS.

I shall be greatly obliged to you, if you will mention it.

CYNISCUS.

It is the custom, I think, for all the dead to drink of the water of Lethe?

RHADAMANTHUS.

Yes.

CYNISCUS.

I would have him alone exempted.

RHADAMANTHUS.

Why?

CYNISCUS.

It will be a moſt grievous torture to recollect what he has been above, to think of his power on earth, to recount his pleaſures paſt.

RHADAMANTHUS.

I agree to it. Let this be his ſentence; that he be taken hence to Tantalus [n], and there chained, and everlaſtingly remember the tranſactions of his paſt life.

[n] Tantalus was one of thoſe perſons, who cannot *fare well without crying roaſt meat*. After dining with the gods, his betters, he blabbed out all that paſſed amongſt his idle companions; for which he was puniſhed with a perpetual longing to dine again.

THE
DREAM;
OR,
The COBLER and his COCK.

On the Comforts of POVERTY.

THE DREAM[a]:

OR,

The COBLER and his COCK.

MICYLLUS.

A PLAGUE take your screaming throat! It is a very hard case that I may not even dream of being happy, but must have my ears pierced with the squalling of a spiteful cock, be roused from my delightful riches, and hurried back to poverty, more hateful still than even thy hideous scream! and yet as far as I

[a] This has been well translated by Sir Henry Sheers, who left out what he did not like, as D'Ablancourt had done before him.

can conjecture from the great stillness of the air, and from my not feeling the bitter cold, which is an infallible token of approaching day; it is not yet midnight. By such superabundant vigilance, one would imagine he guarded the golden fleece they talk of; or what occasion for his crowing all night long? But I will spoil his sport, depend upon it. As soon as it is day-light, and I can lay hold of him, he shall have my good wishes with a good stick, I assure him!

COCK.

My good master, I thought I should have done you a piece of service by waking you thus early. I am sure the earlier you rise, the more time you have for work: and, if you would get up in time, you might, before sun-rise, earn something towards a breakfast, by the repair of an old shoe. However, since for riches in your sleep, you are contented to starve awake, go on and prosper: I will disturb your golden dreams no more, but be as mute as a fish.

MICYLLUS.

Have mercy upon us! the cock talks!

COCK.

COCK.

What, is that such a wonder?

MICYLLUS.

Wonder? ay, surely; I hope it forebodes no harm to me.

COCK.

Indeed, master, you will pardon me; but I cannot help thinking you a very illiterate fellow, totally unread in the works of Homer. Homer, Sir, informs us, that a [p] Steed of Achilles, Xanthus by name, bidding adieu to neighing, stopped to make a speech in the middle of the battle. Nor was he contented to utter plain prose, as I do: verse alone would serve his turn, in which he proceeded like a very orderly prophet. Meanwhile not one of his audience was enough surprized to invoke the averter of evils, as you are pleased to do. What do you think of a speech made by the keel of the ship Argo? The beech of Dodona spoke articulately, and foretold things to come. I suppose you never saw any [q] Oxhides creep,

[p] Hom. Il. xix. ver. 404.
[q] Hom. Od. xii.

or heard the lowing of the flesh, when it was half roasted, and pierced with a spit. Surely it cannot be deemed extraordinary for me to speak, who am so intimate with Mercury, the most eloquent gossip of all the gods; and who besides have the honour of living with Micyllus. However, be that as it will, if you will solemnly promise me not to mention it, I will explain to you this wonderful faculty of mine.

MICYLLUS.

If I truly am awake, and you are really talking to me, I beg you will tell me how it comes to pass. You need not make me swear secrecy; for, if I should relate the story of this night's adventure, nobody could believe it.

COCK.

You have heard nothing to wonder at yet. But perhaps you may be somewhat surprized, when you are told, that I, who thus appear to you a cock, was once a man.

MICYLLUS.

I have heard such a story. There was formerly one Alectryon [r], a namesake of yours,

[r] *Alectryon* in Greek signifies a cock.

who was a young man greatly in favour with Mars, being his confident in his amours, and the constant companion of his jollity. Whenever Mars paid Venus a visit, he took Alectryon along with him; and being sadly afraid lest Phœbus should see and tell Vulcan of him, he used to leave his friend without at the door, to give notice of the enemy's approach. But, the youth happening to fall asleep, and of course being off his guard, the whole affair was discovered. The lovers had gone to rest, confiding in their centinel; and never perceived when Phœbus stood by them. Vulcan, having had his lesson from him, caught them napping, and secured them both in a net, which he had provided for that purpose. Mars afterwards, in a passion, transformed Alectryon into a cock, still retaining his arms and crest. His offspring to this very day, to make amends for the old miscarriage, are sure to be awake, and give notice of the sun's rising, long before it happens.

COCK.

That is an old story, with which I have nothing to do. Mine is a late affair, and quite different

M MICYL-

MICYLLUS.

How was it then? I long to know.

COCK.

Have you never heard of one Pythagoras?

MICYLLUS.

You mean the impertinent Sophist, who forbade the eating of flesh, and of beans (which I think the best eating in the word); and who enjoined a continual silence for five years together.

COCK.

He was Euphorbus, before he was Pythagoras.

MICYLLUS.

Ay, they say he was a great conjurer.

COCK.

Forbear your abuse, my good master, and speak with moderation of what you so little understand: I am that very Pythagoras.

MICYL-

MICYLLUS.

A cock a philosopher! more wonderful still! Explain yourself, son of Mnesarchus [s]. From a man, you became a bird; from a Samian, a Tanagræan [t]! I must beg your pardon for some little defect of faith: I think I have already discovered in you two things very unlike any marks of Pythagoras.

COCK.

What are they?

MICYLLUS.

One is, that you are a noisy prater; whereas Pythagoras enjoined five years silence: and the other is entirely repugnant to his principles. Yesterday having nothing else to give you, I brought you some beans, which, you know, you eagerly picked up, without the least scruple of conscience. Either you lied in calling yourself Pythagoras; or, if you really are Pythagoras, you have violated your own law, and, in eating of beans, are as great a transgressor, according

[s] Pythagoras was the son of Mnesarchus of Samos.
[t] Tanagra was a city of Bœotia, famous for a good breed of fighting cocks.

to what you taught your scholars, as if you had devoured the [u] head of your father.

COCK.

You do not understand, Micyllus, what you talk about. When I was a philosopher, I abstained from beans, as it became me. Now I am a bird, I may fairly indulge my appetite with what is not forbidden a bird.—But, if you will, I will tell you how, from being Pythagoras, I became what I now am; how many modes of life I have passed through, and what was the good and ill attendant on every change.

MICYLLUS.

I beg you will tell me; you cannot please me better. Nay, if it were put to my choice, whether I would have my dream again, or enjoy your conversation, I know not which I should prefer: they are so equally pleasant and precious, so delectable, so desirable.

COCK.

Are you still doating on that empty dream?

[u] Which a bean was thought to resemble.—For many curious reasons inducing Pythagoras to forbid the eating of beans, see Bayle's Dictionary, article PYTHAGORAS.

MICYLLUS.

Yes, be assured, while I have a day to live, I can never forget it. It left a delight in my eyes sweeter than honey; so that I can scarcely keep their lids from closing again to sleep. The tickling your ear with a feather may give you some idea of the sensation I felt.

COCK.

It must needs be a very fond dream, which, in spite of its [w] propensity to fly, does notwithstanding love to pass the boundary of sleep, with sweetness and clearness in the eyes of a man wide awake! I should be very glad to know what it was that did so exceedingly overjoy you.

MICYLLUS.

I am not at all unwilling to relate every circumstance of what is so pleasant to remember.— But when will you favour me with the account of your transmigrations, Pythagoras?

COCK.

When you have given over dreaming, and have wiped off the honey from your eye-lids.

[w] Πτηνς αν.

But first I beg to know whether your dream came flying through the gate of ivory or the gate of horn.

MICYLLUS.

Neither through the one nor the other, Pythagoras.

COCK.

Homer [x] mentions only those two ways.

MICYLLUS.

Pshaw! a foolish old bard! What did he know about dreams? Perhaps indeed the dark dreams of such a blind fellow as he might pass through such beggarly gates. But my most delicious of dreams came through a golden gate, golden itself, encompassed with gold, bringing with it abundance of gold!

COCK.

Good Mr. Midas, let us hear less of gold. Your dream indeed very much resembles his extravagant wish, for it has turned all into gold.

[x] Odyssey xix. imitated by Virgil, Æneid 6.

MICYL.

MICYLLUS.

Oh! Pythagoras, what gold, what abundance of gold did I see! you cannot think how bright it was, how it gliftened!—What is it that Pindar fays in praife of it? do you remember? Firft, you know, he fays " water is the beft thing;" but immediately after he beftows his higheft praifes on gold, as it became him. It is in the beginning of his fineft ode.

COCK.

This is what you mean:

[y] Water excels; but gold is far more bright,
Like fire, that fparkles and expels the night.

MICYLLUS.

The very thing, upon my word! Surely Pindar muft have had a glimpfe of my dream, to fing fo wifely concerning gold. Liften, O moft learned cock, whilft I defcribe it to thee. You know I did not fup at home yefterday. The rich Eucrates, meeting me in the market-place,

[y] This beginning of Pindar's firft ode is fuppofed to be an allufion to the doctrine of Thales, who taught, that water is the firft principle of all things.

invited me to come after bathing, and sup with him, mentioning his hour.

COCK.

I know it very well, having been obliged to fast all day, till you came home late in the evening in your cups, with the five beans. It was but a homely repast for a [z] champion so distinguished at the Olympick games!

MICYLLUS.

After my return from the feast, having given you those beans, I went directly to bed. When, as Homer says,

[a] While I lay slumbering in ambrosial night,
A dream divine appear'd before my sight.

COCK.

But first of all tell me, Micyllus, how matters were ordered at the house of Eucrates, what kind of entertainment you met with, and all

---

[z] Pythagoras, who modestly called himself a philosopher, that is, a lover of wisdom, was also a lover of boxing. He made some considerable improvements in the art, and practised it with success at the Olympick games.

[a] Hom. Il. ii. ver. 56.

that

that paſſed. By theſe means you may ſup over again, chewing the cud of recollection.

MICYLLUS.

I was afraid that the enumeration of ſo many particulars would be troubleſome to you. But, ſince you aſk for my ſtory, you ſhall have it. Having never before, in all my days, been aſked to a rich man's table, by ſome unaccountable good luck, I happened yeſterday to light on Eucrates; when, ſaluting my Lord, as uſual, I withdrew from his preſence, to ſave him the mortification of being ſeen in my ſhabby company. Upon which, "Micyllus, ſays " he, this is my daughter's birth-day, and I " have invited a good many friends upon the " occaſion. But, as I underſtand one of them " is in a bad ſtate of health, and hardly able to " come out, do you [b] bathe yourſelf and " come in his room; unleſs he ſhould ſend " word of being here himſelf, which at preſent " is very doubtful." Hearing this, I made a

[b] Which was uſual before a feaſt or a ſacrifice. Hom, Il. 3. ver. 577.

moſt

most profound obeisance, and took my leave; beseeching all the gods, in their greatest goodness, to send an ague, or pleurisy, or twinging gout, to the sickly gentleman whose place I was invited to fill at the feast. I thought it an age to the time of bathing, looking every moment at the [c] length of the shadow. At last the wished-for hour arrived. Up I got immediately, and set out, being dressed in my best manner, shewing my jacket to the greatest advantage, by turning it inside out. I found a vast number of people at the gate, and, amongst the rest, my sick man, whose place I had expected to have the honour of supplying. He was carried by four persons, and shewed very manifest tokens of not being well. He sighed deeply, coughed, and retched most piteously, looked miserably bloated and wan, and seemed to be about sixty years of age. He was said to be one of those philosophers, who blab out their folly in the ears of youth. His beard was

[c] The Ancients are said to have determined the hour of the day by the length of their shadows. When a man's shadow was ten feet long, it was time to go to supper. Though Micyllus would have been glad of a method more exact, yet he had probably no other dial but himself.

as bushy as a goat's, and stood greatly in need
of a barber. Being blamed by Archibius the
physician, for coming out when he was ill, he
answered, that a philosopher, of all men, could
not neglect his duty, though beset by ten thousand diseases. Besides, added he, Eucrates
might think I slighted his friendship. Not at
all, replied I, but greatly commend you for dying at home by yourself, rather than belch out
your phlegm and your soul at a feast. This
our high-minded philosopher pretended not to
hear. After a while comes Eucrates from the
bath, and seeing Thesmopolis (for that was his
name), " Sir, said he, I am greatly honoured
" by this favour. Though, had you not come,
" you should have fared never the worse; for
" I would have sent you every thing in turn."
Saying this, he went in, giving his hand to
Thesmopolis, who was supported by servants.
I was preparing to sneak off; when, turning
about, and seeing me very melancholy, after
much wavering and consideration, " Come, Mi-
" cyllus, said he, you shall stay too, notwith-
" standing: I can make room for you, by send-
" ing my boy into the women's apartment, to
" sup

"sup with his mother." I go quickly in upon this, in rather a better situation of mind than the disappointed wolf; though ashamed to think myself the cause of shutting out his son from the feast. When the time was come, about half a dozen very stout young men, with much ado, hoisted up Thesmopolis, and put him in his place, bolstering him up with pillows on either side, that he might continue in the situation in which they set him, and hold out as long as possible. Then, as nobody else would endure to sit next him [d], that place fell to my share. Then we fell to work! O Pythagoras, there was such a supper! such a variety of dainties! all silver and gold! the cups were of gold! the servants were so fine! and then we had musick too, and comical fellows to make a body laugh! In short, but for one provoking circumstance, nothing in life could have been more delicious. What I mean was the plaguy Thesmopolis, who vexed me to the very heart with his tedious nonsense concerning

[d] Gesner thinks, that ὁμοτραπεζοι not only implies lolling together on the same couch (according to the well-known custom at meals) but also making use of the same trencher,
some-

something called virtue. He did me the favour to teach me, that two negatives make one affirmative, and that, when it is day, it is not night. Sometimes he said I had [*e*] horns; and ran over a long string of learned cant, which I would most willingly have excused him; for he so interrupted the pleasure of the feast, that there was no hearing the musick for him. Such was our banquet.

COCK.

Not the pleasantest to you, Micyllus, whose hard fate placed you with that old dotard.

MICYLLUS.

But now for my dream.—I thought that Eucrates, who has no child, was going to die; that he sent for me; and that, after making his will, in which he appointed me heir of all, he did die. Immediately I entered upon his possessions, gold and silver without end, which flowed upon me like a stream! Every thing else, his fine clothes, his tables, his cups, his servants, all, all were mine. I got into a chariot

[*e*] These horns allude to the captious argumentation then in use, and have nothing to do with the modern jest.

drawn

drawn by white horses, and, in the laziest attitude imaginable, was gazed on and envied by all. They ran before me, rode about me, followed me in swarms. Arrayed in the gorgeous attire of Eucrates, with a number of monstrous rings, quite sufficient for [*f*] sixteen fingers, I ordered a sumptuous feast for the entertainment of my friends. My friends were come, the supper was got, the wine sparkled. I was drinking the golden goblet of friendship to every one present, and the desert was serving up; when on a sudden thy ill-timed squalling broke up the company, threw down the tables, and gave my riches to the winds. Now do you think I had reason to be angry? Oh! how glad would I have been to have enjoyed that dear dream for three whole nights together!

COCK.

What, are you so greatly enamoured with wealth, Micyllus? and do you think that gold is the only thing which can make a man happy?

[*f*] Eight rings on the fingers were not uncommon. See Icaro-menippus.

MICYLLUS.

I am not the only one of that opinion, Pythagoras. You yourself, when [g] Euphorbus, going out to fight against the Græcians, braided your curls with gold and silver; though in war every body knows it is better to carry a piece of cold iron than a ringlet of yellow wire. However, you thought good to face your danger with golden locks. And it was for that reason, I imagine, that Homer said you had hair like the Graces; because it was crisped and twisted with gold and silver. For doubtless the precious metal much improved its value, as well as added to its beauty and lustre. Nor is it any wonder that thou, O son of Panthus, shouldest honour gold. We know very well that the father of gods and men, the son of Saturn and Rhea, being smitten with an Argolick [b] maid, when he could think of nothing more lovely to transform himself into, or

[g] Hom. Il. xvii.

[b] Acrisius, king of Argi, having been told by an Oracle, that he was to be slain by his grandson, shut up his daughter Danaë in a chamber of brass, a citadel not impervious to the amorous Jupiter.

more

more likely to conquer the guards of her father; went through the tiles in a shower of gold, and obtained the defired accefs to his charmer. What more can be faid on the fubject? How infinite are its ufes! He, who has money, has beauty, and wifdom, and ftrength, and honour, and glory. In one moment, by virtue of money, obfcurity and meannefs are turned into fplendour and fame. You know my neighbour and fellow-craft, Simon. It is not long ago that he fupped with me, in the Saturnalia. I gave him broth and two flices of faufage.

COCK.

Yes; I know him, the little flat-nofed fellow, who ftole our earthen pitcher, the only one we had. I faw him carry it off under his arm after fupper.

MICYLLUS.

And fo he, who invoked fo many gods and goddeffes, was the thief all the while! But pray why did not you fcream as loud as poffible, and make a difcovery, when you faw us robbed of our fubftance?

COCK.

COCK.

I crowed, which is all that was then in my power.—But what of Simon? I thought you had something to say of him.

MICYLLUS.

He had a cousin excessively rich, named Drimulus. This man, while he lived, never bestowed on Simon one single obolus; and no wonder, for he could not find in his heart to bestow any thing upon himself. However, on his lately dying, Simon being heir at law, every thing came to him. And now the poor dirty ragged wretch, who would have given one of his eyes for the privilege of licking a plate, is clothed in purple and violet, has his servants, his equipage, his golden cups, his ivory-footed tables; is adored by every one, and is above even looking at me. Seeing him lately, I thought it was but manners to speak: Your most humble servant, Simon, said I. Upon which he must needs be angry truly, and, calling to his people, " Tell that beggar-fellow, said he, " not to clip my name: I am not Simon, but

"Simonides [*i*]."—But the higheſt affair is, that the women are all in love with him. By turns he is prudiſh, coquettiſh, contemptuous, fond, and fickle. Some poor things are driven to diſtraction, and proteſt that without him life is a burden. You ſee how many fine things gold can do! It transforms into a beau the ug-. lieſt fellow in nature. It has all the virtue of the Ceſtus [*k*] of Venus. You remember

[*l*] O beauteous gold, beſt boon to mortals given! and

'Tis gold ſupreme, that ſways all human things.— But pray what made you laugh?

COCK.

I laughed at your ignorance of the condition of the rich: I find you have embraced the vulgar error. But the truth is, they are much more wretched than you are. I have

[*i*] "Which was the name of a famous poet," ſays a commentator. In ſaying which, he ſays nothing at all to the purpoſe. The Ancients, when they grew rich and great, lengthened their names like the Moderns, though not exactly in the ſame manner.

[*k*] A Girdle, which Juno borrowed formerly, and which anſwered her purpoſe. Hom. Il. xiv.

[*l*] Euripides.

been

been often poor, and often rich; I have tried every situation in life, and speak from experience. You will be as good a judge of all these particulars by and by.

MICYLLUS.

Very well, Sir.—But now let me hear of your several changes, and how you are affected with the remembrance of each.

COCK.

With all my heart. And know this beforehand, that I never saw any man happier than you.

MICYLLUS.

Oh! Sir, your humble servant! You are heartily welcome to my happiness; and much good may it do you! You should not jeer an old friend, left he should be provoked to give you as good as you bring.—But tell me all your story, beginning at Euphorbus, how you afterwards were transformed into Pythagoras, and so on, till in due time you became a cock. In such various modes of existence you must have beheld and encountered a great variety of incidents.

COCK.

As to my soul flying originally down from Apollo, to do penance on earth in the body of a man, that would be a tedious tale to recount; and besides it is neither proper for me to relate, nor for you to hear. But when I was Euphorbus—

MICYLLUS.

Pray, wonderful Sir, before you go any farther, have I too gone through such changes? I would fain know who I was before this cobler that I am now.

COCK.

Gone through such changes? Ay, certainly.

MICYLLUS..

Can you tell me then what I was? I long to know.

COCK.

COCK.

You were an Indian [*m*] Emmet, employed in scratching up gold.

MICYLLUS.

What a blockhead was I, not to bring a few scrapings into this state of coblership, to buy victuals with!—But pray what am I to be next? I suppose you can tell that too. If it is any thing good, I will get up directly and hang myself on your perch.

COCK.

That is a knowledge, which thou canst not obtain.—But, as I was going to say, when I was Euphorbus, being slain by Menelaus in the Trojan war, after some time I became Pythagoras. In the mean time I continued without any settled habitation, till Mnesarchus provided me one.

MICYLLUS.

But you had victuals and drink?

[*m*] These Indian Emmets, according to Herodotus, are about the size of a middling dog. They differ also from other pismires in throwing up hills of gold. Herod. p. 128.

COCK.

No; it is only the body that requires such aid.

MICYLLUS.

Well, but the affairs of Troy—were they as Homer represents them?

COCK.

My dear Sir, how should Homer know any thing of the affairs of Troy, who was all the time a camel in Bactria? You may depend upon this, that things are greatly exaggerated: Ajax was not so broad-shouldered, nor Helen so fair, as people imagine. I saw indeed a woman with a long white neck, like the daughter of a swan; but she was very old, almost as old as Hecuba [n]. Theseus first carried her off, and had her at Aphidnæ. He was contemporary with Hercules, by whom Troy was first taken, in the age of our fathers. I was told this by Panthus, who remembered, when a little boy, to have seen Hercules.

[n] According to this account Helen must have been about threescore, when her beauty was so extremely bewitching. See Bayle's Dictionary.

MICYL.

MICYLLUS.

But what of Achilles? was he so great in every respect? or is it all a fable?

COCK.

I was not acquainted with him, and can say but little on the subject: you know I was not on the side of the Greeks. But as for his friend Patroclus, it was my fortune to [o] dispatch him, which I easily effected by running him through with a spear.

MICYLLUS.

After which Menelaus did your business with still greater ease. But enough of this. I want to hear something of Pythagoras.

COCK.

To give you my character in few words, I was a sophist (since the truth must be told); yet notwithstanding a man of real learning, and skilled in the most liberal arts. I travelled into Egypt to confer with the wise men. I entered the holy recesses, and read the books of

[o] This is not strictly Homerical. Euphorbus indeed wounded Patroclus, but Hector slew him, Il. xvi.

Orus

Orus and Isis. After that I returned into Italy; and the Greeks, who lived there, were so struck with my doctrine, that they revered me as a God.

MICYLLUS.

I had heard all this before; and also that you were believed to revive after death, and that you sometimes shewed a golden thigh.—But pray resolve me this: how came it into your head to make a law against eating flesh and beans?

COCK.

Pray, Micyllus, do not ask me.

MICYLLUS.

Why not?

COCK.

I am ashamed to tell you.

MICYLLUS.

Why should you be so reserved with me your friend? For I will no longer pretend to be your master.

COCK,

COCK.

In fact I had no solid, no reasonable motive at all. But I saw, that, if my institutions contained nothing new and uncommon, I should miss of the admiration of mankind, which is constantly bestowed on what is far-fetched and little known. I therefore determined to surprize the world with something mysterious, which should be guessed at by all, but understood by none; like the ambiguous uncertainty of an oracle.

MICYLLUS.

Do you consider that you are making a fool of me, and playing the same game over again, which you did with the people of Croton, Metapontium, and Tarentum, and the rest of your dumb disciples, who adored the very prints of your feet?—But, when you put off Pythagoras, what form did you next assume?

COCK.

I then became Aspasia, the harlot of Miletus.

MICYLLUS.

Oh! for shame! Pythagoras a female! Then, my good Sir, there was a time when you resembled

sembled a hen more than you do now. You lay no eggs at prefent. You remember, Afpafia, being acquainted with Pericles. You were with child by him. You then carded and fpun, Pythagoras, and acted in all refpects like a woman.

COCK.

What you fay is all very true. But it is no more than Tirefias, and Cœneus the fon of Elatus, did before me. So that whatever reproaches you caft upon me will fall quite as heavy upon them.

MICYLLUS.

Well, but which did you find the pleafanter life of the two, to be a man, or to be the miftrefs of Pericles?

COCK.

You afk a queftion, which Tirefias found it inconvenient to anfwer.

MICYLLUS.

Though you do not think proper to explain yourfelf on that fubject, Euripides has done it
for

for you, who says, he had rather thrice bear a shield than once a child.

COCK.

I will put you in mind of this conversation by and by, Micyllus, when you are in childbed. For, as ages go round, you too are likely to be a woman, and more than once or twice.

MICYLLUS.

Go! Do you think all men Milesians or Samians? They say [p] Pythagoras was very handsome. There is a certain story of a monarch— But after Aspasia, what were you then? a man, or a woman?

COCK.

I was Crates the Cynick.

MICYLLUS.

My stars! what a change! from a whore to a philosopher!

COCK.

Then I was a king, then a beggar, and then a lord, then a horse, then a jackdaw, then a

[p] See Diogenes Laertius.

frog, and a thousand other things which it would tire you to hear. Then I was a cock. I have been often one. I like it. In this station I have served many very different masters, kings and beggars, rich and poor. At present I am a domestick of yours. Every day of my life I laugh to see you weeping and wailing on account of your poverty, admiring the rich, because you are ignorant of their concerns. If you did but know what they feel, you would laugh at your own folly, in imagining that a man must be happy, because he has wealth.

MICYLLUS.

Well then, Pythagoras, or whatever else you like best to be called, for I would not make confusion by a variety of names—

COCK.

It signifies little what you call me, whether Euphorbus, or Pythagoras, or Aspasia, or Crates, which are all the same. Though I should like best to be called what I now am. With so many reversions of souls, I am not a despicable bird.

MICYL-

MICYLLUS.

Since then you have had experience of almost every state of life, explain to me, good Sir, what there is peculiar to wealth, and what to poverty; that I may be a better judge of what you say, when you assert that I am happier than those who are richer.

COCK.

Only consider, Micyllus. In the first place you have no great occasion to trouble your head about war. For, when you are told of the enemy's approach, you are neither afraid for your fields, nor your pleasure grounds; you neither dread their treading down your flowers, nor their destroying your vines: all that you have to do, on hearing the alarm, is only to look out for an opportunity of marching off with whole bones. But the rich, besides the concern for their personal safety, cannot but feel the most cutting anguish, when they behold from the city walls whatever they possessed in the country round ravaged and laid waste. If money is required for the exigencies of state,

whence

whence can it be expected but from them alone? If an attack is to be made on the enemy, who will follow unless they lead? If the honour be their's, so is the danger. You, with your willow shield, can easily bestir yourself, and provide for your safety; and, when the General makes the oblation after a victory, you are always ready to be at the feast. In the time of peace, you, who are one of the people, assume your consequence. You enter the assembly, and domineer over the rich; while they, in fear and dread, are glad to be friends with you at any rate. They provide baths, and games, and shews, and every thing to soothe you. You, a most rigid critic and censor, with all the haughtiness of power, sometimes condescend not even to speak to them. Nay, when to your high mightiness it seems meet, you scruple not to stone them; and, if you are very angry indeed, to confiscate their estates. Meanwhile you neither dread craft nor violence. Your gold tempts no midnight spoiler. You are not tormented with long reckonings; you avoid bad debts, employ no rascally steward, nor are distracted with a multiplicity of cares. In the evening,

evening, when your work is done, and you have earned your seven oboli, you have your choice of indulgences. After bathing, you exhilarate your spirits with an anchovy, or a herring, or a few onions, or what you like best. Your good humour then flows out in many a good old song, and many a precious scrap of philosophy in happy alliance with poverty. This hearty way of life gives a bloom to your cheeks, and strength to your limbs, with a contempt of frost and snow. Alert and active with constant labour, you chearfully encounter with difficulties, which others would tremble to think of. With regard to diseases, none of the dangerous ones ever invades you. In case of a slight fever, you are your own physician, and soon drive it away; for fevers and hunger agree not long together. They fly from him, who takes no draughts besides draughts of water. But the wretched votaries of luxury, from what that is bad can they escape? gouts, consumptions, peripneumonies, dropsies — are they not all the children of intemperance? Those who, like Icarus, soar aloft, and venture too near the sun, forgetting the wax which
fastens

fastens their wings, soon come tumbling down head foremost into the sea. While the true disciple of Dædalus, contented on this side the skies, and even flying so low as to be now and then wetted with a wave, bids fair to fly in safety.

MICYLLUS.

I suppose you mean a reasonable and moderate man.

COCK.

How wretched are the wrecks of ambition! Think how the wings of Crœsus were clipped by the Persians, and what an abject figure he was on the funeral pile! Dionysius, from being the tyrant of a mighty realm, became the monarch of a school, in which he issued edicts on the royal art of spelling!

MICYLLUS.

But tell me, good Cock, when you were a king (for such I understand you have been), what did you think of that life? Were you not perfectly happy, in having attained the summit of human felicity?

COCK.

COCK.

Put me not in mind of such unspeakable wretchedness. That I appeared happy is true; but alas! it was but appearance! my mind was devoured with unceasing anxiety.

MICYLLUS.

Impossible! I know not how to believe you.

COCK.

I was king of a very extensive, fruitful, and populous country, containing many cities of most admirable beauty, with many navigable rivers, and many excellent seaports. I had a vast army, cavalry well disciplined; a large body of guards, galleys for pleasure, money without end, curious works in gold; and in short every article in the farce of state. Whenever I appeared abroad, they adored me as a God, pushing and squeezing one another to see me. Some would climb up to the tops of houses, to be blessed with a full view of my equipage, my royal robe, my diadem, my retinue. I all this while was the secret prey of ten thousand tortures. Their admiration might be forgiven,

as the effect of ignorance. But alas! poor me!
Though in their eyes I was a Colossus, in my
own opinion I was little and pitiful enough.
Observe the outside of a fine figure of Jupiter
or Neptune, fashioned in gold or ivory by the
nice hand of Phidias, or Myron, or Praxiteles;
you cannot but admire it. In the right hand
you are struck with the exact representation of
a thunderbolt or a trident [*q*]. But, if once
you get a peep at the inside, your admiration
abates, and you discover that all is not gold
that glistens. You there see certain bars and
wedges and nails driven every way, pieces of
wood, pins, pitch, and clay, and whatever else
can destroy all form and figure. I mention not
the mice and other vermin that occasionally
have a colony there. Such a thing is a kingdom.

MICYLLUS.

But you have not specified the clay and the
wedges and the bars, which deform the inte-

[*q*] There are many passages in this translation, to which
it was not difficult to give a more modern turn. But a
translation of such passages without any marks of the original idea would be no translation at all.

rior parts of government. I am sure, to ride about in state, to command so many thousands with a nod, and to be worshiped like a deity, are privileges very great and very inviting; of which your Colossus was a very proper illustration. Now finish your comparison, and tell me what you have to counterbalance all these fine things.

COCK.

It is not easy, Micyllus, to determine what to begin with. I shall mention fears, anxieties, suspicions, surrounding hatred, restless intrigue, short and broken slumbers disturbed with horrid dreams, roving imaginations, evil expectations, perpetual attention on business without end, trials, expeditions, edicts, compacts, consultations. Exposed continually to all these, do you think it possible to enjoy any comfort even in a dream? When one man must be constant watch for all, occupied in ten thousand things at once.

[r] The son of Atreus found no sweets in sleep;
Since cares in him eternal vigils keep:

[r] Hom. Il. x. ver. 3.

Homer

Homer says this of him, at a time, when every other Greek was snoring.—The Lydian king is afflicted with a dumb son. The Persian monarch is deserted by Clearchus, who raises troops for Cyrus. Another is vexed with Dion, who concerts measures with Syracuse. The praises of Parmenio are grievous to another. Ptolomy troubles Perdiccas. Seleucus plagues Ptolomy. To have a treacherous mistress, to hear the rumour of an intended revolt, to observe three or four of the guards circulating an important whisper, always to suspect those most who are their most familiar friends as persons from whom nothing good is to be expected—this last is wretchedness indeed. One king is poisoned by his son. Another dies in an unnatural embrace. By some similar death they commonly fall.

MICYLLUS.

Fie upon it! what an account you give! At this rate it is a safer kind of life to stoop over an old shoe, than to drink courtesy [1] and

[1] —— nulla aconita bibuntur
Fictilibus. Juvenal x. ver. 25.
—— No doubt the poor man's draughts control;
He dreads no poison in his homely bowl.
Dryden's translation.
poison

poison out of a golden goblet. If indeed my knife slips in cutting my leather, I am in danger of cutting my finger. But they, it appears, have not even their banquets unstained with blood, but are for ever beset with all manner of mischief. A king, when he falls, is hardly in better plight than one of the prostrate actors in a tragedy, of which you must have seen many. Perhaps he represented Cecrops, or Sisyphus, or Telephus, with his diadem, and ivory-hilted sword, with his streaming hair, and embroidered robe: but if, as it often happens, the great man meets with a tumble upon the stage, he is the laughing-stock of every spectator: his mask and diadem are cracked, not only his royal but his real head is broken; his legs unprotected by his train tell a beggarly tale of rags, displaying ugly buskins ill buckled, and as badly fitting his feet. You see, my good Sir, that you have taught me to make a simile.—Well, such was the condition of majesty. But, when you were a horse, or a dog, or a fish, or a frog, how then?

COCK.

At present we have not time to discuss that point. I will only observe in general, that man, encompassed as he alone is with præternatural desires and fantastical wants, has the least quiet of any animal under the sun. I believe you will never see a horse a tax-gatherer, a frog a sycophant, a jackdaw a sophist, a gnat a cook, a cock a pathick: such illustrious occupations are followed by man alone.

MICYLLUS.

No doubt what you say is exactly right. But (I beg your pardon) in my early youth I longed to be rich, and cannot get it out of my head to this very day. This very moment I think I see all the gold of my dream; and, from my soul, I envy that rascally Simon, who battens in such plenty.

COCK.

I can cure you of that this very night. Only come along with me. I will take you to that Simon, and to the houses of other rich men, that you may be a witness of their situation.

MICYLLUS.

How can you do that, when the doors are shut? would you make a housebreaker of me?

COCK.

No. But Mercury, whose bird I am, has bestowed on me this peculiar privilege, that, if any person takes the longest soft crooked feather of my tail —

MICYLLUS.

You have two just alike.

COCK.

I say, if I pluck off this feather on the right, whatever person I think fit to give it to, will have during my pleasure the power of opening any door, and of seeing whatever is within, while himself is invisible.

MICYLLUS.

Upon my word I did not know that you were a conjurer. But I am glad of it with all my heart. Do but lend me the feather, and you shall see Simon's whole estate brought hither in a minute; I will manage that. So he may once more be reduced to live upon leather.

COCK.

That cannot be. You are not authorized to steal by means of my feather; and Mercury has commanded me, if any such attempt should be made, to crow out " Thieves!" as loud as possible.

MICYLLUS.

A very likely thing indeed! that Mercury, who is a thief himself, should dislike the profession in another! But however let us go. I will keep my fingers from the gold, if possible.

COCK.

But first pluck off the feather. Hold! you have got them both.

MICYLLUS.

It is better so: both sides of your tail being alike, you will not be disfigured, nor limp in your gait.

COCK.

Well, let it be so. But shall we visit Simon first, or some other rich man?

MICYL-

MICYLLUS.

Let us go to Simon's by all means. Since my gentleman grew rich, he has doubled his name: nothing less than four syllables will serve him.—But this is the house; what must be done now?

COCK.

Put the feather to the lock.

MICYLLUS.

Oh wonderful! the door flies open, as with a key!

COCK.

Step in. Do not you see him wide awake, poring over his accompts?

MICYLLUS.

Yes; I see him sitting over a little dim thirsty wick of a candle. He is as pale as ashes! quite gone to a shadow. What, is it care that pines him so? I never heard of any other distemper he had.

COCK.

Hush! let us hear what he is about.

SIMON.

SIMON.

Stay—the seventy talents buried under the bed—they are safe—nobody saw. I wish I could say as much of the sixteen hidden under the manger. The groom Sosylus certainly saw me. Yes, yes, he is become very fond of the stable of late; though careless enough before, and very little in love with labour. That is not all I have been robbed of, I dare say. Or, how came Tibius by such a relishing dish yesterday? It seems too, that he laid out [/] five drachmas in an ear-ring for his wife. All that they spend must be the property of poor me. Some rascal or other will break into my house as sure as can be: I wish my plate was safe. There are many malicious persons who would be glad of an opportunity to ruin me; and none more than my neighbour Micyllus.

MICYLLUS.

Yes, to be sure, I am a little like yourself at present; for I have tucked a dish or two under my arm, which I intend to carry off.

[/] 3l. = ¼d.

COCK.

COCK.

Hush! Micyllus, he will discover us.

SIMON.

It is quite necessary for me to keep awake, and be upon my guard. I will go round the whole house.—Hah! who is here? What, you have broken into my house—but I see you!—oh! it is only a pillar; very well!—I will take up my money again, and count it once more, to see that it is all right.—Hark! I hear a noise again.—there is somebody! woe is me! beset and betrayed and attacked on all sides!—Where is my dagger?—Let me but catch you!—Softly now; let me bury my gold again.

COCK.

You see what a comfortable life Simon's is.—But let us go to some other, while a little of the night remains.

MICYLLUS.

Wretched indeed! may all my enemies be as rich as he!—I will just give him a good slap on the face, by way of taking leave.

SIMON.

SIMON.

Who is that? alack! alack! I am wounded! I am robbed! I am robbed!

MICYLLUS.

Mayest thou lament and watch and pine till thou art as pale as thy gold!—If you think fit, we will now visit Gniphon the usurer: he lives just by.—His door is open to our hands.

COCK.

He too, you see, is sleepless with care, and, with withered fingers, is casting up his interest. Yet how soon must he leave all, to be perhaps a moth, a gnat, or a fly!

MICYLLUS.

I see the poor fool. He is already very little more than one of the diminutive things you mention; he is so wasted with computation.—But let us go to another.

COCK.

To your friend Eucrates, if you will. Behold! the door is open, so that we may go in directly.

MICYL.

MICYLLUS.

All this was mine alas! how little a while ago!

COCK.

Are you dreaming still? There! do you see that abominable fellow, that old fellow, what he is about?

MICYLLUS.

Infamous unnatural wretch!—His wife is with the cook in a different part of the house, in a very unseemly situation.

COCK.

Now do you long to be the heir of Eucrates? would you desire to succeed to what you have seen?

MICYLLUS.

Rather let me perish with hunger than have any resemblance to him! Farewell gold! farewell feasting! Let all my estate consist of two oboli, rather than live in dread of being robbed by my servants!

COCK.

COCK.

But come, it is almost day-break; let us go home. You may see the remainder another time.

ICARO.

ICARO-MENIPPUS.

A GENERAL INVECTIVE

AGAINST

Gods, Men, Manners, and Opinions.

ICARO-MENIPPUS.

MENIPPUS and his **FRIEND.**

MENIPPUS.

FROM the earth to the moon, which was my first stage [*u*], three thousand stadia! from thence up to the sun about [*w*] five hundred parasangs! from thence to heaven itself and the lofty citadel of Jove, about as far as a good nimble eagle can fly in a day!

FRIEND.

In the name of wonder, Menippus, what are all these grand things you are measuring and

---

[*u*] 375 miles. This is somewhat different from a later account, which makes the distance about 60 semidiameters of the earth.

[*w*] 1875 miles, supposing the Persian measure parasang equal to 30 stadia.

mutter-

muttering about? I have followed you this half hour, and hear of nothing but suns and moons and stations and parasangs, and other outlandish stuff.

MENIPPUS.

Wonder not at my aerial sublimity of style. I was going over the heads of a late extraordinary expedition.

FRIEND.

So, like the [x] Phœnicians, you traced your way with stars!

MENIPPUS.

No, truly; but I travelled in the stars.

FRIEND.

On my word you have had a comfortable nap, if you have dreamt over whole parasangs.

[x] The Phœnicians were very skilful navigators. Without the aid of the compass, they found their way to Cornwall many ages ago, where they left several Greek words, which remain there to this day. The inhabitants of that country (as is supposed) not submitting patiently to be plundered of their tin, these adventurers thought it very uncivil, and carried home such a character of them as Horace afterwards expressed by Britannos hospitibus feros.

MENIPPUS.

Pr'ythee talk not of dreaming to me, who am just come from Jupiter.

FRIEND.

What? Menippus from heaven? from Jupiter?

MENIPPUS.

From the great Jove himself this very day. What wonders have I heard and seen! If you do not choose to credit what I say, that very circumstance adds to the extravagance of my delight in having been happy beyond belief.

FRIEND.

Thou divine and Olympian Menippus, how should I, a mere earth-begotten mortal, presume to doubt what is brought from beyond the clouds, by one admitted into the society of Homer's celestials? But pray, Sir, if it is not too much trouble, tell me how you got up. Where could you find a ladder long enough? For I hardly think you handsome enough to be flown away with by the eagle, for a cup-bearer, as Ganymede was.

MENIPPUS.

Very fine! You may be just as merry as you please, Sir, with my wonderful ascent. But I wanted none of your expedients of ladders or eagles; for I had wings of my own.

FRIEND.

You far exceed Dædalus: I was quite ignorant of your having commenced kite or jackdaw.

MENIPPUS.

When you mention Dædalus, you are not very wide of the mark; for I put in practice his original invention.

FRIEND.

A most undaunted hero indeed! And had you no apprehensions of a fall any where into the water? Then we might have had the Menippean sea, as well as the Icarian.

MENIPPUS.

I had no fears about the matter. The wings of Icarus were fastened with wax; so that the first approach to the sun must necessarily disjoin

join them, and give him a fall. But mine was a better contrivance.

FRIEND.

I should be glad to comprehend you. For somehow or other I begin to imagine there is some reality in what you say.

MENIPPUS.

I will tell you. I caught a huge eagle and a sturdy vulture, and having fairly cut off their wings—but, if you have leisure to hear me, I will begin with my motives for the undertaking, and tell you every circumstance of the story.

FRIEND.

I am all attention. By all that is friendly, do not think of leaving me hanging by the ears in the air.

MENIPPUS.

By no means. Having examined into the affairs of this life, I discovered all human things to be ridiculous, mean, and uncertain. Accordingly, with a most hearty contempt of riches, honour, and power, and all that belongs to them, I betook myself to better employment, endeavouring to lift up my eyes and contemplate the universe. And first I could not tell what to make of what the wife men call the world. I could not discover the cause and manner of its existence, whence it derived its beginning, nor what was to be its end. And, the more I descended to particulars, my difficulties were the more increased. I saw the stars scattered at random through the sky, and longed to know something of the sun. The appearances of the moon were beyond my comprehension; to some occult cause I attributed the multiplicity of her phases. The impetuous activity of thunder and lightning, the descending rain, snow, and hail, were what I could not trace out, nor conjecture the cause of. In this state of anxious uncertainty, I thought my best way would be to consult the learned philosophers. For certainly, thought I, they must be able to tell me the exact truth of every thing. Having therefore fixed on the most knowing of them (as I judged from the sourness of their looks, their pale complexions, and long beards) paying down a large sum of money,

money, and promising a great deal more, when I should attain the summit of sapience, I desired to be taught the constitution of the universe and the high flights of sermocination. For indeed to me they seemed to use a language they had learned in heaven. But alas! instead of delivering me from my former ignorance, they only served every day to increase it, filling my ears with principles, final causes, atoms, vacuums, matter, forms, and other jargon equally intelligible. But what was the least of all to be endured was, that, though no two of these men are agreed in any one point, but each is perpetually at war with all the rest; yet every one insisted on my implicit faith in him, and utter rejection of all the rest.

FRIEND.

It is strange that men so wise should differ so from one another.

MENIPPUS.

You must laugh, were you to hear the impudence of these fellows. A set of earth-born mortals, not at all superior to their brother-reptiles, just as blind as their neighbours, nay some of them literally so through age and idleness, do notwithstanding undertake to prescribe boundaries to heaven, to measure the sun's orb, to tread over the head of the moon; and, as if they were just dropped from the stars, to tell us their size and shape. Who, though perhaps they know not the distance from Megara to Athens with any tolerable exactness, yet have the assurance to mention the number of cubits between the sun and moon, to teach us the height of the atmosphere, the depth of the sea, the precise orbit of the earth; and, with all the parade of circles, triangles, squares, and globes, to make us believe they measure to an inch, even heaven itself. Is it not the very last degree of pride and folly, that, in treating of matters so obscure, nothing is ever proposed as conjecture, but each endeavours to outdo the other's presumption, and is ready to take an oath, that the sun is a lump of fire, that the moon is inhabited, that the sun, as with a bucket in a well, draws up water out of the sea, and gives drink to all the stars. You see what a clashing of sentiments there is amongst them, which indeed goes through every part of their

their doctrine. For first they cannot agree in opinion concerning the world. Some will have it without beginning and incorruptible; while others have ventured not only to find out a maker for it, but also his manner of going to work [y]. These last are truly admirable: they have found out the divine architect of the universe, but proceed not to tell us whence he came, or where he was stationed, when he fabricated the world; before which we find it impossible to imagine either time or place.

FRIEND.

Bold venders of legerdemain!

MENIPPUS.

Dear Sir, what would you say, were I to recount their disputes about ideas, incorporeal essences, finite, and infinite? About these last there is a sharp conflict, some circumscribing the universe, others allowing it no boundaries at all. Some maintain a plurality of worlds, and have no charity for those who think dif-

[y] Whether the nonsense of this atheistical sophistry is to be attributed to Lucian or Menippus, is an enquiry not worth making.

ferently.

ferently. One, not the most peaceable man in the world, affirms, that war is the parent of all things. It is needless to mention their various opinions concerning the gods. Some make number their divinity. Others swear by dogs, and geese, and plane-trees. Some, rejecting all other gods, bestow universal empire on [z] one: so that it grieved me to hear of such a dearth of divinities. Others, more liberal, allow us great plenty, of different ranks and orders. Some teach, that the deity is without body or shape; but others tell a different tale. Several of them scruple not to affirm, that the gods take no manner of concern in our affairs, nor ever trouble their heads about us. Like the mutes in a play, they are as free from all care, as an old man past his labour. Others, surpassing all the rest, leave the world to wag as it will, and believe in no gods at all. When I had heard all this, though there was no refusing full credit to men who talked so big, and were so well bearded, yet I

[z] Εν μονῳ, uni soli. Had the honest gentleman, who rendered this "the sun alone," relied on the simple Greek, he would not have been betrayed by the duplicity of the Latin *soli*.

knew not where to incline myself, to avoid falling on what had been overturned by another. Thus irresolute, and vibrating this way and that way, as [a] Homer describes it, I despaired of meeting with any certain information upon earth. The only way to get rid of my doubts, I thought, would be to take a flight, if possible, into heaven. My hopes of accomplishing this were supplied by my own ardent desire, and encouraged by Æsop, the author of the story-book, who makes nothing of mounting up eagles and beetles, and even [b] camels. As to my obtaining a pair of wings of my own natural growth, I saw no possibility of that: but, if I should put on those of a vulture or eagle (which alone seemed equal to the weight) I might chance to succeed. Accordingly, the birds being caught, I carefully cut off the right wing of the eagle, and the left of the vulture;

[a] Hom. Od. ix. ver. 302.
[b] There is a fable quoted as Æsop's, in his Life by Planudes, which, Moses du Soul thinks, would have been referred to here, if it had been extant in Lucian's time. There was something curious in that Monk Planudes: he remembered circumstances which had never existed, and forgot those which had.

which

which I fastened to my shoulders with stout leathern thongs, and, laying hold of the extremities with my hands, by the assistance of them and my feet, I tried to raise myself up, half hopping and half flying, on the tips of my toes, as you have seen a goose do. As I improved in flying, I grew bolder; and, having got upon the citadel, I threw myself down headlong upon the theatre. Flying in this manner without danger, I began to think of going upwards; till, from Parnes, or Hymettus, I flew to Geranea; and from thence to Acrocorinthus; then over Pholoë, and Erymanthus, and as far as Taygetus. When I was grown somewhat perfect, and thought myself no longer a chicken, nor incapable of a bold attempt, I got upon Olympus; from whence, having laid in a stock of provisions, in the most commodious manner I could, I made the best of my way directly towards heaven. At first I was a little giddy with the height, but afterwards I bore it well enough. When I had left the clouds far behind, and was now got to the moon, I felt myself grow weary, and especially in the left wing, which was the vulture's. Landing

ing therefore, and sitting down, I rested myself; while, like Jupiter in [c] Homer, I looked down one while on the land of Thrace, famous for horse-flesh; another while, on Mysia. Afterwards, as the whim took me, I contemplated Greece, Persia, and India; and was filled with variety of delight.

FRIEND.

I beg you will not grudge me one tittle of your travels, but favour me with every observation you had occasion to make. I expect to hear a great deal concerning the figure of the earth, and of all things upon it, and how they appeared to you looking down from such a distance.

MENIPPUS.

Right, Sir. Get up then, as fast as you can, into the moon; and, travelling with me in your imagination, observe the situation of all earthly things. First of all, think that you see a very little earth, much less than the moon; so little, that, bending myself downwards, I wondered what was become of the huge mountains,

[c] Hom. Il. xiii. ver. 4.

and

and the vast sea. As sure as you are there, if I had not espied the Colossus of Rhodes, and the watch-tower of Pharos, the earth would have quite escaped me. But the vast height of these buildings, with the reflection of the sun from the ocean, convinced me, that what I saw was the earth. And, when I had once got a steady sight, all human life appeared plainly before me; not only nations and cities, but individual sailors, and soldiers, and husband-men, and lawyers, and women, and wild animals [d], all that the fruitful earth maintains.

FRIEND.

What you say is incredible and contradictory. Just now you would not have been able to find out the earth, diminished by the immense distance to a point, had it not been owing to the Colossus; but behold! all at once, like another Lynceus, you nicely discern every thing it contains, man, and beast, and, as I suppose, the nest of a gnat!

MENIPPUS.

I am obliged to you for your hint: I had like to have forgot a very important circum-

[d] Hom. Od. xi. ver. 308.

stance.

stance. When I had made out the earth, but could not distinguish any thing else, my sight falling far short of the distance, I was exceedingly concerned, and at my wit's end. Being much dejected, and almost ready to weep, the sage Empedocles presented himself to me, exceedingly scorched, all over ashes, and black as a collier. I was much troubled, I confess, at the sight of him, taking him for some deity of the moon; but he assured me that I was mistaken.

"Upon my honest word I am no God [*e*]."
"I am the naturalist, Empedocles. When I
"leaped into the crater of Ætna, the vapour
"forced me up hither, where I traverse the
"air, and live upon dew. My business at pre-
"sent is, to free you from your concern. I
"perceive, Sir, you are troubled at not seeing
"distinctly what is doing upon earth." You are very kind, said I, good Empedocles; and, as soon as I go down again to Greece, I will not forget to make you a libation in the chimney-corner, and three times to adore you, with open mouth, at every new moon. "By En-
"dymion, answered he, I come not to you with
"any mercenary view! I am sorry to see you

[*e*] Hom. Od. xvi. ver. 187.

"so

" so dejected: do you know how to improve
" your sight?" Not I truly, replied I, unless
you could remove this cloud from my eyes:
for I am almost blind. " You stand in no
" need of my assistance, said he, having brought
" with you from the earth what you want."
What is that, said I, for I declare I know not
what you mean? " Do not you know, said he,
" that you have got on the right wing of an
" eagle?" Yes, said I; but what have wings
to do with eyes? " An eagle, said he, is the
" most sharp-sighted of all living creatures;
" and he that can bear to look at the sun with-
" out winking, is accounted the royal bird,
" of the * genuine breed." I have heard so,
said I; and am sorry, that, before I came hither, I did not pull out my own eyes, and fix
those of an eagle in the sockets. I am but
half equipped for my journey, and, for want
of regalia, no better than a bastard, or out-cast.
" But, said he, it is your own fault, if you
" have not one royal eye. For, if you will
" rise a little, holding your vulture's wing, and

* This method of resolving doubts concerning legitimacy
was practised with success by certain eagles of Pliny's acquaintance. Nat. Hist. lib. x.

" shaking

"shaking the other, you will find, in propor"tion, that your right eye will become piercing;
"while the other, which belongs to the worse
"side, will grow dim without remedy." Oh!
said I, I shall be contented to have one eagle's
eye: that will serve my turn. For I have observed, that carpenters, using only one eye,
manage their line so much the better. Having
said this, he withdrew a little, and vanished insensibly into smoke; whilst I was preparing to
follow his directions. No sooner had I begun
to flap my wing, than a great light shone all
around me, and I plainly discovered what before was imperceptible. Looking down upon
earth, I distinctly beheld cities and men; I
saw what they were doing, and not only in the
open air, but in their own houses, where they
thought themselves safe from all observation.
I saw Ptolomey with his incestuous sister; I
saw the son of Lysimachus plotting against his
father; I saw Antiochus, the son of Seleucus,
amorously nodding to Stratonice, his mother
in law; I saw Alexander, the Thessalian, murdered by his wife; I saw Antigonus polluting
his daughter in law; I saw Attalus poisoned
by

by his son; I saw Arsaces murdering his mistress, and Arbaces the eunuch drawing his sword against Arsaces. Spartinus, the Mede, was dragged out from the banquet, by the guards; after getting a black eye with a golden cup. In this manner went on all manner of wickedness in the palaces of Libya, of Scythia, and of Thrace; adulteries, murders, assassinations, robberies, perjuries! men in the utmost confusion, betrayed by their most intimate friends!—Though the affairs of princes thus engaged my attention, those of their subjects were in full as bad a situation. I saw Hermodorus, the Epicurean, forswear himself for a thousand drachmas; Agathocles, the stoick, going to law with his scholar for wages; Clinias, the orator, stealing a phial from the temple of Esculapius; Hierophilus, the cynick, asleep in a brothel. Housebreakers, usurers, duns, plaintiffs, and defendants, made up the rest of the motley shew.

FRIEND.

I wish, Menippus, you would be particular, in relating what must have so highly delighted you.

MENIPPUS.

Indeed, my good friend, you must excuse exact order and minuteness; since it was difficult to get even a cursory view of every thing. My account must be as general as that of Homer, when he describes the [*f*] shield of Achilles, in one part of which were feasts and weddings, in another assemblies and courts of justice. Here was a man sacrificing, there was one mourning. The Getæ seemed a people engaged in war, and wandering Scythia rode in a waggon. Turning a little the other way, I beheld the Ægyptians at plow, the Phœnicians making bargains, the Cilicians robbing, the Lacedæmonians whipping, the Athenians at law. Think of this hodge-podge of human affairs, and you will allow it impossible for me to have got a very clear idea of every particular. It was like every man singing his own song at a concert: and you may imagine the odd effect of every one's exerting himself to the utmost, in justice to his own tune.

[*f*] Hom. Il. xviii.

FRIEND.

FRIEND.

Ridiculous confusion, to be sure!

MENIPPUS.

Just so proceed all the performers upon earth! and such is the ingenious discord of life! so jars the concert, where nothing is uniform! till the master of the ceremonies pushes all off the stage, and declares the entertainment at an end! From that moment all are hushed alike, and cease their disorderly song. But certainly in the diversified theatre of life, where all things differ, all things agree in provoking disdain. But what diverted me very highly, was to see them contending about the boundaries of their land, thinking it a great thing to have a Sicyonian farm, or one of Marathon near Oenoë, or to possess a thousand Acharnian acres: meanwhile, with my four fingers, I thought I could have covered all Greece; of which Attica was a diminutive spot indeed! I could not but wonder what those rich men could find to be so proud of, when the largest of their estates hardly exceeded an atom of Epicurus. When I cast my eyes down upon Peloponnesus and Cynouria,

Cynouria, I could not help thinking for what a pitiful speck, scarce bigger than a lentil, so many Argives and Spartans fell in one day! but to see a man proud of his money, or his finery, eight rings, and four cups, ye gods! one is ready to burst! when Pangæus, with all its mines, was hardly more than a millet-seed!

FRIEND.

Oh! you have been a happy fellow! But tell me, pr'ythee, how the cities and the men looked, when you were so high above them.

MENIPPUS.

I suppose you have seen an ant-hill, where some are wriggling round and round, some going out, others coming home; one dragging out dung, one running in with a bean-shell, another with half a grain of wheat: in that manner live men, a mixt multitude of architects, demagogues, statesmen, fidlers, and philosophers. If this way of elucidating my argument requires any apology, I refer you to the ancient traditions of Thessaly; where you will find, that the warlike race of Myrmidons were

were originally ants.—When I had seen all I could, and laughed to my heart's content, I shook my feathers, and took my flight towards the

[g] House of deities, the court of Jove.

I had hardly ascended a hundred paces, when the moon, with a feminine voice, called after me, " I wish you a good journey, Menippus! " Will you do me a small favour above?" If you have nothing heavy to carry, said I, I beg you will command me. " Only a message, an-
" swered she; I only want you to present a
" humble petition to Jupiter. I am pestered
" beyond all enduring by a generation of men,
" who call themselves philosophers; who, hav-
" ing no business of their own, must needs be
" troubling their heads about me. They ques-
" tion me who I am, and how big I am, and
" for what reason I appear sometimes to have
" lost a little piece of my cheek, and sometimes
" a full half of my face. Some say, that I
" am inhabited; others, that I hang over the
" sea for a looking-glass. Whatever proceeds
" from their own muddy brains they place to

[g] Hom. Il. i. ver. 222.

" my-

"my account. Then they will have it, that
"mine is a bastard-light, and not honestly come
"by, since it proceeds from my brother the
"sun, with whom they wickedly endeavour to
"set me at variance. As for him, they say,
"he is a stone, or a mass of fire. And yet,
"notwithstanding the liberties they take with
"me, I have scorned to divulge the midnight
"practices of these grave personages, so re-
"spectable by day-light, and so admired by
"fools. For I think it unbecoming to ex-
"pose what passes in secret. When I catch
"them in adultery, or theft, or any other deed
"of darkness, I immediately withdraw behind
"a cloud, that I may not expose to unhallow-
"ed eyes what could so little be expected in
"men advanced in years, of such enormous
"beards, and such extraordinary pretensions to
"virtue. Yet, as if all this forbearance of
"mine signified nothing, they are continually
"pulling me in pieces, and misusing me every
"way they can think of. Night is my wit-
"ness, that I have often had it in my head to
"remove to some far distant tract, beyond the
"reach of their impertinent tongues. Pray

"do

"do not forget to tell all this to Jupiter, and
"assure him, that there is absolutely no living
"here for me, unless he agrees to break the
"necks of these naturalists, stop up the mouths
"of the dialecticks, demolish the porch, set
"fire to the academy, and make an end of
"the peripateticks. If he would do this, I
"might be at peace, and keep my dimensions
"to myself, which they are now every day pre-
"tending to measure." Very well, said I, I
will execute your commission. Immediately I
set forwards for heaven,

[b] Where marks of neither man nor beast appear.
Presently the moon looked a little diminutive
thing, and the earth under her disappeared.
Leaving the sun upon my right, and flying
through the stars, on the third day I saw the
end of my journey. At first I thought of an
immediate admittance, supposing I should pass
unnoticed, being half an eagle; and knowing
the eagle to be an old favourite of Jupiter's.
Then again I considered the probability of
being detected, from having the wing of a vulture. Judging it best therefore to avoid the

[b] Hom. Od. ii. ver. 98.

danger,

danger, I stept up and knocked at the door. Presently comes Mercury, who, having enquired my name, ran back to tell Jupiter; and I was soon introduced, all pale and trembling, to a general assembly of the gods, who looked almost as much concerned as myself. This unexpected visit of mine had not a little disconcerted them; and they were beginning to doubt, whether it would not become fashionable for mortals to fly to heaven, since I had set the example. Jupiter, screwing up his features, and looking like a [*i*] Titan, said,

Who art thou? how descended? of what place?
I was thunderstruck with his voice, and ready to die with fear. After some time, being a little come to myself, I told him honestly every particular from the beginning, of my conceiving a desire to be acquainted with sublime things, of my consulting the philosophers, of their gross contradictions, how I was distracted and driven to despair, of my subsequent project, how I had contrived my wings, and in

---

[*i*] Τιτανώδις. To look like a Titan, is to look big. The Titans might well be thought to look big, who had the assurance to attempt dethroning their uncle Jupiter.

short

short every circumstance that happened in my way to heaven. Last of all, I delivered my message from the moon. Jupiter then opened his brows a little, and, smiling, observed, that it was in vain to talk of Othus and Ephialtes, when even Menippus had dared to climb the skies. However, at present, says he, I beg you to accept of such entertainment as this place affords; and I will dismiss you to-morrow, after we have conferred together on the occasion of your coming. Saying this, he got up, and walked to a kind of whispering-gallery, where he finds it most convenient to hear the vows of mortals, for which this was the hour of audience. Going along, he was pleased to ask many questions concerning matters below. He enquired how wheat sold in Greece, whether we had been greatly pinched by the severity of the last winter, and whether the cabbage wanted rain. He asked me, whether any now remained of the race of [k] Phidias, why the Athenians had omitted the feasts of Jupiter so many years, whether they had any thoughts

[k] Phidias was famous for making an ivory image of Jupiter Olympius; which might occasion this enquiry.

of finishing his temple on mount Olympus, and
whether the villains had been taken, who pil-
fered his shrine at Dodona. When I had answered these questions, " Pr'ythee, Menippus, says
" Jupiter, what sentiments do men entertain con-
" cerning me?" What sentiments, said I, but the
most dutiful and affectionate! that you are the
king of all the gods. " You joke, said he; I
" know better: they are fond of novelty.
" There was a time indeed when they esteem-
" ed me a prophet, and a physician, and every
" thing: not a market, not a street, was without
" its Jupiter. Pisa and Dodona were seen
" glittering from afar. Scarcely could I open
" mine eyes for the smoke of incessant sacri-
" fice. But, since Apollo has set up the trade
" of fortune-telling at Delphi, Æsculapius has
" kept an apothecary's shop at Pergamos, Ben-
" dis has had her temple in Thrace, Anubis
" in Ægypt, and Diana at Ephesus; all the
" world runs after them, hold a hundred meet-
" ings, and slaughter many a hundred bulls to
" their praise: while I, a poor superannuated
" old fellow, must be contented with the abun-
" dant honour of being recollected once in five
" years

"years at Olympia. You see, my altars are
"colder than the institutes of Plato, or the
"syllogisms of Chrysippus."—With such conversation as this we passed away the time, till we came to the place, where he was to sit and hear petitions. There were trap-doors placed in order, with covers to them, resembling draw-wells, and close by each was placed a golden throne. Seating himself by the first of these apertures, Jupiter took up the lid, and listened. Various and manifold were the prayers, that were sent up from all parts of the world at once. For I too applied my head to the vent, and heard. One prayed very ardently to possess a kingdom, another was no less eager for onions and garlick; one begged of Jupiter to take to himself the soul of his father, another urged the like request in behalf of his wife. One man begged of Jupiter not to mention his project of murdering his brother; some desired success in law-suits, others crowns at the Olympick games. Of the people at sea, one requested a north wind, another a south wind. The farmer prayed for rain, the fuller for sun-shine. Jupiter listeded attentively,

tively, and confidered every thing well, but did not always promife.

[*l*] This would his godfhip grant, and that refufe. All reafonable demands were admitted through the opening, and laid up on the right hand; others he puffed away down to earth, nor would fuffer them to come near him. There was a particular cafe, which puzzled him. Of two men with equal pretenfions, as promifing equal offerings, each requefted what was directly contrary to, and incompatible with, the defire of the other. So that Jupiter was in that fufpence of the Academicks, which makes it impoffible to come to a refolution; and was as much a fceptick as [*m*] Pyrrho himfelf.—When he had done with thefe petitioners, he removed to the next throne, at the fecond opening; and, bending his head, heard great plenty of oaths. Having knocked out the brains of the perjur-

[*l*] Hom. Il. xvi. ver. 250.
[*m*] Pyrrho lived with his fifter, and ufed to carry chickens to market, and fweep the houfe, and wafh the difhes. His temper was not eafily irritated; for, when he talked of his learning, he was quite indifferent whether any body liftened to him or not. See Diog. Laer.

ed Hermodorus, he went to the next place, where business relating to augury and divination is transacted. From thence he crossed over to the window, where the ascending smoke made known to him the name of every one employed in offering sacrifice. These too being dispatched, he next proceeded to give orders to the Winds and Weather. Let there be rain, says he, in Scythia to-day; lightning in Libya; snow in Greece; let Boreas bluster in Lydia, and let Notus be at rest; let the West-wind roll the Adriatick; and let a thousand bushels of hail, or thereabouts, be scattered in Cappadocia.—At last, every thing being settled, we repaired to the banqueting-house; for it was now supper-time. Mercury took me under his care, and seated me by Pan, and the Corybantes, and Attis, and Sabazius, those upstart divinities, of doubtful title. Ceres served us with bread, Bacchus with wine, Hercules with butcher's meat; Venus supplied us with myrtle-berries, and Neptune with anchovies. Now and then I could steal a taste of nectar and ambrosia. For you must know, Ganymede is
a good-

a good-natured fellow, and, when Jupiter was looking another way, he two or three times brought me a tumbler. The gods neither eat bread nor drink wine, as [n] Homer says, and as I myself observed, who had a much better opportunity of knowing than he. Yet they feast on ambrosia, and grow jolly over their nectar. But they are never better pleased than with the relishing smoke of a sacrifice, or the warm steam of blood fresh from their altars. During supper we were entertained with Apollo playing on his harp, and the saraband of Silenus. The Muses got up, and sang the [o] Theogony of Hesiod, and the first ode of Pindar. When every body was tolerably well moistened, we went to rest, in our places.

[p] Now gods and men their labouring eye-lids close,
And all but mine are shut in soft repose.

For I had many thoughts to keep me awake. Amongst other perplexing doubts, I could not guess why Apollo's beard was not yet grown

[n] Hom. Il. v. ver. 341.
[o] Not the whole of it. It contains 1021 verses, a great deal too much for convivial joy to attend to.
[p] Hom. Il. ii. ver. 1.

in so many years; and I wondered how Night got admittance into heaven, where the sun is a constant guest. At last however I slumbered a little. Jupiter, getting up early the next morning, called a full house, and spoke as follows: " The stranger, who came hither yester-
" day, has occasioned my calling you together.
" Indeed I had long thought of consulting with
" you about those philosophers; but being
" now greatly provoked with accounts of them
" sent from the moon, I am resolved to defer
" it no longer. A set of frothy fellows have
" lately over-run the age, who are lazy, quar-
" relsome, vain, passionate, ravenous, foolish,
" conceited, foul-mouthed, an [*q*] idle burden
" to the earth. They have split themselves into
" Sects, and devised various labyrinths of ra-
" tiocination. Some call themselves Stoicks,
" others Academicks, others Epicureans, and
" others Peripateticks; not to mention other
" appellations much more ridiculous. En-
" trenching themselves behind the venerable
" name of virtue, exalting their eye-brows, and
" stroking their beards, they conceal their vile

[*q*] Ετωσιον αχθος αρουρης. Hom. Il. xviii. ver. 104.

" designs

"designs in a counterfeit habit, and strut about,
"as you have seen one of the stalkers in tra-
"gedy, from whom, if you strip off his mask
"and his embroidered robe, what is left of him
"is a contemptible poor wretch hired for
"[r] seven drachmæ to play the fool. Yet
"they have the assurance to despise all other
"men, tell monstrous stories of the gods, gull
"credulous young men, vaunt of their com-
"mon-place virtue, vend their dear ambiguity,
"ever full of the praises of moderation and
"temperance, and ever decrying all riches and
"all pleasure, before those who are fools
"enough to believe them. But, were you to
"see them by themselves what they really are,
"you would be astonished: their luxury, their
"debauchery, their sordid avarice, is beyond all
"bounds. What is most provoking of all,
"though themselves do no one earthly thing
"of use, neither publick nor private, but are
"altogether supernumerary and good for no-
"thing,

"[s] Useless in council, as unfit for arms;

[r] 4 s. 6½ d.
[s] Hom. Il. ii. ver. 202.

"yet

"yet are they for ever finding fault with other
"people, induſtriouſly heaping up all the viru-
"lence and ſcandal they can rake together on
"their neighbours. And he is the greateſt
"man amongſt them, who is beſt qualified, by
"impudence and clamour, for every kind of
"abuſe. If you ſhould take the liberty of aſk-
"ing ſuch a fellow: " I beſeech you, Sir, in
"the name of all the gods, what are you good
"for? what do you contribute to the emolu-
"ment of human life?"—If he anſwers truly,
"he muſt ſay: " Why ſhould I go to ſea, or
"follow the plough, or ſerve in the war, or
"exerciſe any trade? ſince, to make a noiſe,
"to go dirty, to plunge into cold water, to go
"barefooted in winter, and, like Momus, to
"cenſure the actions of others, anſwers my pur-
"poſe much better? If a rich man indulges
"himſelf in good eating, or keeps a miſtreſs,
"I am never at eaſe, till I have an opportunity
"of tattling. But a friend or companion may
"be ſick, and in want of help, without my
"knowing any thing of the matter."—You ſee,
"ye gods, what kind of cattle they are!—But
"the Epicureans are the ſaucieſt of all, not
"ſparing

" sparing even us. They affirm, that the gods
" take no cognizance of human affairs, nor ever
" regard what passes in the world. Is it not
" then high time to look about you? For, if
" once men should come into this opinion, I
" fancy you may starve for them. Who, do
" you think, will offer a sacrifice, which, he
" believes, will do him no good? As to the
" complaints from the moon, you all heard the
" stranger relate them yesterday. I would have
" you consider the matter, and resolve on some-
" thing most useful to mankind, with the
" greatest safety to yourselves." When Jupiter
had ended, a murmur ran through the whole
assembly, and all cried out at once, [*t*] " Blast
" them! burn them! dash them to pieces!
" down with them to hell! down with them
" among the rebels!" Jupiter, having again
commanded silence, said: " Things shall be as
" you wish; they and their gibberish shall pe-
" rish together. But nobody can be punished

[*t*] Such language does not seem altogether becoming the place. Tacitus indeed says, that a great noise and uproar were not uncommon in the Roman Senate: but one might have expected better manners in a cœlestial assembly.

R 2   " at

"at present; for you know it is holiday-time,
"and I have ordered a vacation of four months.
"But in the beginning of next spring the vil-
"lains shall feel my bolt."

[r] He spake, his nodding brows announcing fate.

"As to Menippus, let Mercury take him home
"to earth. But let his wings be clipped, that
"we may have no more of his company
"here." Saying this, he dismissed the assembly. Mercury, laying hold of my right ear, yesterday in the afternoon landed me in the [w] Ceramicus. Now, my friend, I have told you all, all from heaven. I am going with the good news to the philosophers walking in the [x] Pœcile.

[v] Hom. Il. i. ver. 528.

[w] A burial-place at Athens for such as had been slain in war.

[x] Pœcile, ποικίλη, *various*, was the portico or piazza, which took its name from being adorned with various pictures of Athenian battles. In porticibus deambulantes disputabant philosophi. Cicero de Oratore, iii.

OF EXERCISES [y].

[z] ANACHARSIS a Scythian,

AND

SOLON the Lawgiver of ATHENS.

[y] See a dissertation on the Olympick games by Gilbert West, Esq;

[z] Anacharsis was the only philosopher of his country. He improved himself by travel, and, at his return home, was put to death by the king his brother, for endeavouring to introduce the Athenian laws. The king perhaps did not believe Anacharsis, when he said, that laws were like cobwebs, which caught little flies, but could not hold wasps and hornets. Cicero, Tusc. Quæst. v.

OF EXERCISES.

ANACHARSIS.

WHAT is it these young men are about? They twist themselves round each other, endeavour to trip one another up, stop one another's breath, and roll and tumble in the dirt like so many hogs. When they first stripped off their clothes (for I was standing by) they greased and rubbed one another very lovingly; after which, all at once, without any quarrel that I could perceive, they began to push and butt one against the other, like a couple of rams. Mind him there! he has got his antagonist off his legs, and dashed him against the ground! He throws himself upon him, sinks him deeper into the mud, and will not suffer him to get up. Then, with his knees on his belly, and his elbow in his throat, he almost suffocates the poor wretch, who pats his shoulder, beseeching him, I suppose, not to stifle him outright. They are not at all careful to keep either their oil or themselves from the dirt. One cannot but smile to see them as slippery as eels, all over grease and sweat and mire. There are others, in the open air, who do the same thing, except that, before they engage, they sprinkle one another, like cocks, with sand. The sand, I suppose, dries up the lubricity of the skin, and gives them a faster hold. Standing upright, covered with dust, behold! how they beat and kick one another! That poor fellow looks ready to spit out his teeth, together with a mouthful of blood and sand, which he has got by a blow on his face. The [a] magistrate yonder does not interfere to end the dispute. (I suppose the gentleman in purple is a magistrate.) So far from discouraging it, he praises him who gave the blow. Others are in violent agitation, and, without

[a] The Gymnasiarch, or President of the Exercises.

removing

removing from their place, have all the trouble of running, leaping, jumping, and kicking the air. I should be glad to know what can possibly be the use of all this. For my part, I take them to be mad, and shall not easily be convinced of the contrary.

SOLON.

I do not at all wonder, Anacharsis, at what you say. These things must needs appear very strange to a Scythian; as no doubt many of your customs would to a Greek. But believe me, Sir, what you see is not the effect of madness; nor is it a mischievous disposition, which prompts these young men to beat one another, and cover one another with dirt, or sand. This useful exercise is not unpleasant, and contributes greatly to the strength of the body. I dare say, if you should continue any considerable time in Greece (as I hope you will) you would become one of these dirty dusty fellows yourself, and find both the pleasure and advantage of it.

ANA-

ANACHARSIS.

And what may your prizes be?

SOLON.

In the Olympick games a garland of wild olive, in the Isthmian one of pine leaves, in the Nemean one of parsley, in the Pythian sacred apples; and we Athenians, in our Panathenæan games, give the oil of Minerva's olive. What do you laugh at, Anacharsis? do you think such rewards inconsiderable?

ANACHARSIS.

By no means, Sir: I think the rewards are exceedingly proper, befitting the bounty of the magnificent donors, and suited to the extravagant ambition of those who obtain them! It is richly worth while, to be sure, to labour so hard, to be so shockingly abused, to endanger limbs and life too, for an apple or a bit of parsley! for, most confessedly, without all this kicking, beating, and bemiring, it would be impossible to get apples, pine leaves, or parsley!

SOLON.

SOLON.

My good Sir, it is not the rewards themselves, which we consider; otherwise than as they are tokens of victory and distinction, for which the candidates of Fame are contented to be kicked, and bear every hardship. For glory is not the portion of the lazy, but the delightful end of long and laborious difficulty.

ANACHARSIS.

To shew their garlands and their bruises, to be praised by those who pitied them, to be repaid for their troubles with apples and parsley, must make them very happy!

SOLON.

You are a stranger. But you will come into a proper way of thinking, when once you have been present at our publick spectacles, where you will see such crowds of people, the theatres filled with admiring thousands, praising the combatants, and extolling the victorious to the very skies.

ANACHARSIS.

The matter is so much the worse, that the indignity is not to be suffered in the sight of

only

only two or three, but in a publick assembly of the people, who are all eye-witnesses to the happiness of him who streams with blood, and has the breath squeezed out of his body! For such is the felicity attendant on victory. But, in my country, Solon, whoever was to strike a citizen, or throw him down, or tear his clothes, would be severely punished for it by the magistrate; although the affront were given in presence of only a few, and not in such crowded theatres as those of Isthmus or Olympia. From my heart I pity your combatants, considering how much they endure. And I no less admire the madness of the spectators, who, you say, consist of the most respectable from all parts; that they should abandon their necessary concerns, and find leisure to frequent these festivals. I cannot conceive the pleasure of seeing men beating and wounding one another, dashing to the ground, and mangling the bodies one of another.

SOLON.

I only wish, Anacharsis, that you had an opportunity of being present at the Olympick, or Isthmian,

Isthmian, or Panathenæan Games: you would then see our reasons for retaining such customs, and being fond of such amusements, as no description can give you an adequate idea of. If you were once seated amongst the spectators, and beheld the accomplishments of the combatants, the beauty of their persons, their admirable health and vigour, their astonishing skill, their invincible strength, their boldness, their ambition, their ardour of resolution, their unremitting eagerness for victory—were you to see all this, I am very sure, that you would never have done praising, shouting, and applauding.

ANACHARSIS.

Could any man living, on such an occasion, refrain from laughter and derision? All the virtues, O Solon, that you have enumerated, all that health, all that vigour, all that beauty, and all that boldness, are well disposed of truly! You must derive great advantages from such qualities so employed, when neither your country is endangered, your lands laid waste, your families injured, nor your friends oppressed! Seriously I look upon these distinguished personages in a very ridiculous light. I shall never forbear

forbear laughing, when I think of men bearing
so many hardships, struggling with so many
difficulties, disfiguring their fine persons with
mud and sand, and freely putting up with black
eyes and bloody noses, to obtain the honoura-
ble enjoyment of an apple, or an olive branch.
But have all the combatants these rewards?

SOLON.

No, certainly; only the conqueror.

ANACHARSIS.

And so many are eager to engage in a contest, where the chances are so greatly against
them, and where they know that only one can
have the prize; where all the rest must sit down
with the satisfaction of being soundly beaten
and grievously wounded!

SOLON.

You seem, Anacharsis, to be yet to learn what
constitutes good government: otherwise you
would not think of blaming these excellent institutions. But, if you should ever study the
formation of a state, and the probable means

of

of producing the best citizens, you will then
commend these exercises of ours, and that emulation, which we so much encourage; and you
will see your great mistake, in supposing that
these men have only their labour for their pains.

ANACHARSIS.

I am come, Solon, to your country, as far as
from Scythia, over a prodigious tract of land,
and over the vast and tempestuous Euxine sea,
for no other purpose, but to inform myself of
the laws and manners of the Greeks, and to enquire into the best forms of government; for
which reason I have preferred your friendship
and hospitality to those of all the other Athenians, from your fame as a legislator and moralist, the introducer of useful discipline, and
modeller of the whole commonwealth. You
cannot, I assure you, be more desirous of teaching, than I am of learning. I shall be contented
to sit, without eating or drinking, and greedily
listen as long as your strength and spirits will
enable you to discourse on whatever relates to
government and laws.

SOLON.

SOLON.

It would be impossible to bring you acquainted with every thing at once. But, by attending to one thing after another, you will understand the reasons of our institutions concerning the gods, our parents, our marriages, and so forth. As to what we have thought fit to determine concerning our young men, and how we dispose of them, as soon as they are able to distinguish what is right, being in full strength, and able to bear hardships; I am going to explain that matter to you now, that you may understand why we order these exercises, and our reasons for inuring our youth to toil. Certainly it is not for the mere obtaining of the prizes, which accompany these contests (which fall to the share of but a very few), but that the whole community, as well as these individuals, may be benefited in something of greater consequence. For there is one common pursuit, in which all good citizens are engaged; which, though not for a garland of pine, or olive, or parsley, yet comprehends in it the universal good of mankind; as publick and private liberty, the enjoyment of riches and glory, of established festivals, of domestick security, and, in short, all the good things for which we are wont to supplicate the gods. These are all interwoven in the garland I mean, which is acquired in the contest, to which these labours and these exercises lead the way.

ANACHARSIS.

Truly I wonder, Solon, when you had rewards of such consequence to reckon up, that you should spend any time in descanting on apples, and parsley, and pines, and olives.

SOLON.

Even these you will consider with some respect, when you have heard what I have to say. They derive their origin from the same source, and are inferior parts in that great contest, and of that crown, which confers, as I observed, all human happiness.—But I know not how it has happened, the discourse, transgressing all order, has begun with the transactions of the Isthmus, Olympia, and Nemea. However, since we are both at leisure, and you are so willing to hear,

we

we can easily go back, and deduce from its principles that great contest, which occasions all the rest.

ANACHARSIS.

Undoubtedly it would be best to speak of things in their natural order. By which means I may possibly be soon convinced of my mistake, and think it no longer a laughing matter, to see a man pompous and proud, for having got a garland of olive or parsley. If you will, we will retire into the shade, where we may sit on the benches, undisturbed by the shouts to the wrestlers. Besides, to tell you the truth, I cannot well bear the sun, darting his fierce and fiery rays upon my naked head. For I left my cap at home, because I would not look singular in any thing foreign. But this is the season of the year, when the dogstar (as you call it) rages intolerably, burning and scorching the whole atmosphere; while the sun, being directly over one's head at noon, occasions a degree of heat, which is insupportable. I wonder how an old man like you can bear it without sweating, as I do. Not at all incommoded, you think nor of looking for shelter in the shade, but continue unconcerned in the burning sun.

SOLON.

These insignificant labours, O Anacharsis, these continual tumbles in the mire, these pains in the hot sand, make us proof against the rays of the sun. We want no caps, to keep off the heat.—But let us go. I would not have you place an implicit belief in all I say. Whenever you think me in the wrong, I hope you will put me right, and make no scruple of contradicting me. By this way of proceeding, one of these two consequences must follow.—Either you will be thoroughly convinced, being confuted in all your objections: or I shall recant my mistakes, and learn my political creed anew; by which you will merit the thanks of every Athenian. For the more you reclaim me from my errors, and bring me to a juster way of thinking, the more you will be a benefactor to my country. When that is the case, I shall conceal nothing, nor keep any thing back from the common stock of knowledge; but will address myself to my countrymen: "I have
"com-

"composed, O men of Athens, such laws as I
"thought would be most for the good of the
"state. But this stranger (meaning you,
"Anacharsis), this Scythian, who is a wise man,
"hath compelled me, by dint of argument,
"to change my sentiments, pointing out to
"me other and better laws and institutions than
"my own. It is therefore your part to enrol
"him amongst your benefactors, and erect him
"a brazen statue, near the image of Minerva,
"amongst those illustrious men, from whom
"our Athenian tribes derive their names."
Do not imagine, that the men of Athens will
think it any disgrace to be instructed, though by
a stranger and Barbarian, in what so essentially
concerns the commonwealth.

ANACHARSIS,

I had heard before, that you Athenians are
much addicted to raillery. How should I, a
poor wandering rustick, the unsettled inhabitant
of a waggon, perpetually changing my situation,
who never lived in, never saw a city before
this—how is it possible for me to harangue on
govern-

government, or presume to instruct [b] a people bred in their own soil, a city so ancient, so long happy under the influence of such excellent laws? and especially how can I assume such a character in the presence of Solon, the study of whose life has been to discover by what means a state may flourish, and by what laws and manners the people are rendered happy? It well becomes me in this matter to pay all imaginable deference to you. Though I shall not fail to offer my objections to what may appear less manifest; that, by the removal of them, you may more effectually inform me of what is right. We are now in the shade, out of the reach of the sun; and here is a very good seat on this cold stone. Explain to me therefore in full the effects of Exercise, which your people are inured to from boys; and tell me how clay, and labour, and dust, and tumbling, constitute a great man. This I long to know first: you will teach me other things in their turn. But pray remember that you are speaking to a Barbarian; neither puzzle me with intricacy, nor outrun me with prolixity; lest

[b] Αυτόχθονες, eodem innatos solo quod incolunt. Justin.

I for-

I forget the beginning, before we come to the end.

SOLON.

You will be the best judge of that yourself. Whenever I lose perspicuity, or run away from the argument, you may call me to order, and ask what questions you please. However, I hope, if nothing is said foreign to the purpose, nor inconsistent with the subject, that you will allow me a reasonable length. For even in the court of Areopagus, which decides in capital cases, it has ever been the custom of our country to allow of long speeches. Whenever the court sits for the trial of murder, or wilful maiming, or destroying of property by fire, each party has liberty to speak, the one after the other. Or, if they themselves have not the faculty of making speeches, they may hire others to plead for them. And, as long as they speak to the purpose, they are patiently attended to. But, if any one artfully endeavours to gain over the inclinations of the judges, or to excite pity or indignation by a profusion of oratorial impertinence (which is often attempted by young pleaders),

pleaders), the crier immediately steps forward, and commands silence. It is not permitted them to trifle with the court, nor raise a mist about the cause, to prevent the naked truth from appearing. I now, Anacharsis, constitute you an Areopagite. As long as I speak to the point, and follow the rules of court, you will give me your attention: but, whenever I wander abroad in mood and figure, you will immediately stop my tongue, and restrain me within due bounds; yet so as never to prevent my expatiating at large on what comes within the compass of our design. While we are unmolested by the sun, you can have no great cause to complain, though the discourse should prove none of the shortest. The shade is thick, and we have nothing to do.

ANACHARSIS.

You are right, Solon: I think myself much obliged by your digression concerning the customs of Mars's hill, and the proceedings of those worthy magistrates, who fix their whole attention on the truth. Proceed then; while I, an an Areopagite (for such you have made me), will listen to you, like myself.

SOLON.

In the first place, it will be proper to shew you briefly what we understand by a city and citizens. We consider not a city, as consisting in its edifices, in its walls, temples, and harbours. All these are at best a kind of firm and immovable body, fitted for the reception and security of the people. All power and authority belongs to them. It is the people who fill, order, perfect, and protect the whole; in the same manner as the soul animates every one of us. Upon these principles, we extend our cares, as you may observe, to the body of the city, which we adorn with the most elegant structures within, and secure with the strongest fortifications without. But our first and greatest of all cares is, that the people may have virtuous minds, and strong bodies: such will be of use to each other in peace, and will save and defend the liberty and happiness of the state in war. To accomplish such ends, we commit the

first

first care of their education to [e] mothers, and [e] nurses, and [e] schoolmasters; who, we expect, will teach them what is proper to begin with, and lay the foundation of a liberal turn of mind. But as soon as they begin to perceive the beauty of virtue; when modesty, and a sense of shame, and fear, and a desire to excel, have taken root in their minds; when their bodies are able to endure labour, being more firm and compact; we then alter the discipline and culture both of the mind and body. For we think it not sufficient merely to be born under such circumstances as all others are; unless our bodies and minds are cultivated in such a manner as will conduce most to private and publick advantage. By care and diligence our good dispositions are improved and strengthened, and whatever is amiss is altered for the better. In this we copy the example of the husbandman, who, while his plants are young and tender, covers and secures them from the wind;

---

[e] The superior merit of the nurse constantly bears away the palm from her competitors. It is to the credit of mankind, that no age has been barren of gratitude to so propitious a character. She is seen in the best company, and has had poetical justice done her by Homer, Virgil, and Pope.

but,

but, when the stalk has acquired sufficient firmness, cutting off every superfluous part, he commits them freely to be blown and shaken by every breeze; of which he reaps the advantage. We first excite in their minds a desire of learning musick, and arithmetick; we teach them to write, and read distinctly. As they grow up, we frequently repeat to them the sayings of wise men, the exploits of antiquity, and useful lessons, put into verse, that they may be more easily remembered. Hearing thus of the virtuous and memorable actions of famous men, they are inflamed by degrees with a desire of imitating them; that they too may be celebrated and admired by posterity; like the heroes of old Homer and Hesiod. By and by, when they are of age to be employed in the state, and take upon them the management of publick affairs—but this is digressing. For I intended not at first to shew the manner of exercising the mind: the business was, to let you see the propriety of inuring the bodies of our youths to labour. I therefore enjoin myself silence, without waiting for the crier, or expecting the reprehension of such an Areopagite as you, who,

who, I suppose, are too good-natured to recall me from my wandering.

ANACHARSIS.

What is the reason, Solon, that, in the Areopagus, when a man conceals the most important circumstances in profound silence, the court does not think of punishing him?

SOLON.

I cannot answer your question, without knowing what you mean.

ANACHARSIS.

I mean, that you are passing by the best part of the subject, and what would give me greatest pleasure to hear. Neglecting what belongs to the mind, you would confine your discourse to the labours and exercises of the body; which are matters of less consequence.

SOLON.

Because, Sir, I very well remember what we begun with, and have no desire to overload your memory with too many words. However, I
will

will briefly touch upon that point also. For to
handle it accurately would require a complete
difcourfe. We temper and harmonize their
minds by teaching them the common laws, all
of which are expofed to the publick, who fee
written in large letters the duties they are to
perform, and the vices they are to avoid. We
introduce them to the acquaintance of good
men, fuch as we call Sophifts and [*d*] Philofo-
phers, from whofe converfation they learn to
fpeak properly, to do juftice, to live as becomes
fellow-citizens, to engage in no mean purfuit,
to follow what is good, to forbear every kind of
violence. In the comedies and tragedies,
which are publickly reprefented in the theatre,
we fet before them the virtues and vices of
old times, that they may learn to emulate the
former, and abhor the latter. We allow our
players the liberty of ridiculing and fatirizing
fuch of our citizens as act unworthily of their
character, and are a difgrace to the ftate.
[*e*] Which is done not only on their account,

but

[*d*] A word unknown in Solon's time.

[*e*] The truth is, that Solon was fo far from hoping to
reform men's manners by theatrical reprefentations, that,

when

but for the sake of others. For men, seeing themselves thus exposed to derision, will naturally take care to avoid the occasion of it.

ANACHARSIS.

I believe, Solon, I have seen those tragedians and comedians, which you mention. The former have great heavy shoes half way up their legs, golden bindings on their coats, and have monstrous ugly gaping heads. They talk uncommonly big out of the heads, and stalk about in the shoes with mighty state. It was at the feast of Bacchus, I think, that I saw them. Your comedians were less elevated, made less noise, and walked and talked more like human creatures. But their [*f*] head-pieces were far more ridiculous, and they made the whole theatre laugh. The other lofty beings excited a general sorrow; being pitied, I suppose, on

---

when Thespis the strolling player came to Athens, he would not suffer him to exhibit. Solon had the same opinion of tragedies that another discerning lawgiver had of Gulliver's Travels, which, he said, " was a book full of improbable lies, and for his part, he hardly believed a word of it." Diogenes Laertius, p. 15. Pope's Works, vol. ix. p. 59.

[*f*] See the personae in Sandby's Terence.

account of the heavy clogs, which so miserably encumbered their legs.

SOLON.

The actors were not the objects of pity, my good Sir. The poet, I imagine, produced a detail of some ancient calamitous story; and his mournful diction, aided by the actors, might well occasion the shedding of many tears. Did not you see also some persons playing upon flutes, and others standing in a circle, and singing? Neither the singing nor the piping is without its use. By all such things the mind is sharpened and improved.—Our manner of exercising their bodies, which you seemed desirous to know, is this: As soon as they are grown firm and strong, we strip off their clothes, and expose them fully to the weather; till every season becomes indifferent, and they neither regard the heat of summer, nor the cold of winter. Then, we supple their bodies with oil, which makes them more pliant and vigorous. For it were absurd to suppose, that tanning, which is so useful to a dead hide, should do no good to a living body. Then, by the invention of

of a variety of exercises, for each of which we appoint a master, whether it be boxing, or whatever else, we accustom them to endure toil, we teach them to defy a blow, and be fearless of a wound. Hence arise two very great advantages: our young men enjoy perfect health and strength, and, by never sparing themselves, acquire the greatest contempt of danger. By being used to wrestling, they learn to fall with safety, to get up readily, to push, to grapple, to twist, to squeeze, to lift their adversary from the ground. These things are of great use, but especially in one principal circumstance, that persons trained in this manner become much stronger, and better able to endure hardship. Another advantage far from being inconsiderable is, that, having long been practised in peace, they are always expert in war. Such a man, being engaged with an enemy, will sooner bring him to the ground; or, if he be down himself, will more easily get up again. In all these contests, Anacharsis, we have an eye to real engagements in war. And we cannot but be of opinion, that men prepared in this manner must distinguish themselves in arms. Their naked
bodies

bodies are made supple and active by oil and exercife; they are ftout, and ftrong, light, and dextrous, and fully prepared to over-power the enemy. You can eafily conceive what they muft be in arms, whofe appearance, when naked, ftrikes terror into an enemy; who are neither lumpifhly fat, nor delicately lean; who exhibit not the appearance of women, that pine in the fhade; who do not tremble, and fweat, and pant under a helmet, though the fun exert his meridian power. What would they be fit for, were they to be made uneafy with thirft, or grow faint with duft? were they to fwoon at the fight of blood, and, before they are within reach of the enemy, fall down dead with fear? Our youths look as they fhould do. Their ruddy cheeks are tempered by the rays of the fun. They are full of life, and fire, and manly vigour. Having attained habitual health, being neither loaded with fat, nor withered with the want of it, their bodies are kept in proper order. All hurtful fuperfluities are evaporated by fweat, and nothing is retained but what contributes to ftrength and activity. As the chaff is winnowed from the wheat, fo we clear the

body

body of those redundancies, which would destroy its health and vigour. Hence it is, that they have the best constitutions, and can bear the greatest and most lasting labours; that they rarely sweat, and are very seldom faint. To return to the winnower: if one should set fire to wheat, straw, and chaff; the straw, I dare say, would be gone in a trice; but the corn itself would not take fire but by slow degrees, and without any blaze, requiring a considerable time to smother away, and be entirely consumed. Thus a right constitution of body does not soon submit to labour or disease. Where the inside is in good order, and the outside well fortified, neither heat nor cold can do harm. The superabundant warmth of constitution, acquired by constant exercise, administers such occasional supplies of vigour on any emergency, as are almost invincible. For previous toils and labours do not diminish, but increase the strength, which is roused and excited by motion, like fire under embers. Besides we so accustom our young men to running, that they are able not only to hold out through a long course; but, from their lightness and speed, to perform it

with

with the utmost expedition. They do not run upon hard firm ground, but in deep sand, which sinks under them every moment, and makes it very difficult for them to keep on their feet, where they flip at almost every step. To improve them in leaping, we supply them with [g] leaden weights, which they hold in their hands, and attain such a proficiency by practice, that they are not stopped by a ditch or any such obstacle, but fairly jump over it. They endeavour also to outdo one another in throwing the javelin. You saw in the Gymnasium a round thing made of brass, resembling a small shield, but without any handle or thongs. You tried the weight of it, as it lay before you, and thought it heavy and difficult to be laid hold of, by reason of its smoothness. They toss that up into the air, or straight forwards, as far as possible, every one endeavouring to go beyond all the rest. This exercise strengthens the shoulders, and gives a spring to their limbs. I proceed now to inform you what are the uses of the dust and clay, which you thought so

[g] Something like this may be seen in some parts of England.

ridiculous. In the first place a fall in the soft mud is not attended with danger. And then they become more slippery by sweating in the mire. You may call this the conduct of an eel; but it is neither ridiculous nor useless. It conduces not a little to the strength and pliableness of the muscles; for they must of necessity lay fast hold, or they have no chance of keeping one another from perpetually escaping the gripe. It is no easy matter to hold a man all over oil, and mud, and sweat, flinging and tossing himself on all sides, to get out of your hands. All these things (as I told you before) are of vast use in war, either when you are to carry off a wounded friend from the field, or when you are to seize an enemy and bear him off in your arms. We therefore propose to them immoderate exercises; that, being used to overcome difficulties, they may not be daunted with ordinary occurrences. On the other hand, our reason for exercising them in the dust is, to prevent slipping. For as by much practice in the mud they learn to hold fast their antagonist, in spite of his aptitude to escape, in the sand they learn to get away themselves, when they

they seem caught. The dust receives and restrains the profuse sweat, occasions their strength to hold out, and prevents the evil consequences of exposing the open pores of the body to the wind. Besides, it cleans the body, and clears the skin. I wish I could set before you one of those pale-looking creatures brought up in the shade, and any one of these exercised in the Lycæum; that, after washing off the dust and mire, I might ask you which of the two you would wish to resemble. I know you would at first sight, without any experience of either, determine, that the firmness and strength of a good constitution is to be preferred to a delicate complexion, wasted and dissolved in luxury, and pale from a scarcity of blood, which retires to the inward parts.—Such, Anacharsis, are the exercises, to which we accustom our youth, and by means of which we expect them to be the bulwarks of their country. Under such protection we hope to live in liberty, and vanquish every enemy that shall dare to attack us. By such means we shall be always formidable to the neighbouring nations, the greater part of which will be well contented to pay us tribute.

bute. In peace also we experience the good
effects of these games. Our young men enter
into no vicious emulation: their leisure being
thus employed, they are not mischievous for
want of something to do. The publick weal,
the highest felicity of a state, consists (as I observed)
in having the young men always ready
to engage with alacrity in the most laudable
pursuits, equally prepared for peace and war.

ANACHARSIS.

So, when the enemy approaches, you besmear
yourselves well with oil, make yourselves very
dirty, and march out to box them! They doubtless
run away in a terrible fright, not daring to
open their mouths, lest you should dash in handfuls
of sand; afraid of your jumping round
them, getting upon their backs, twisting your
legs about them, and putting your elbows in
their throats! They may shoot their arrows, and
throw their darts, if they please: but they will
make about as much impression on men full of
blood and well tanned by the sun, as on so many
statues! You are not made of straw, or chaff,
to give way at the first onset! Late, very late,
and

and not till after many grievous wounds, will ye vouchsafe to lose a little blood! Is not this what you mean? Or, perhaps, you will accoutre yourselves in the panoply of your players, and go out to battle with gaping masks, and frightful faces! And I suppose you will put on the high shoes, which will feel light, if you should judge it proper to fly; and by the assistance of which you may make such mighty strides as cannot fail to bring you up with the enemy, if your business should be to pursue!—To be serious, I would have you consider, Solon, whether such curious devices be any more than mere trifles, a suitable occupation for young men who have nothing to do, and are willing to enjoy their idleness. If you think of being free and happy in good earnest, you stand in need of a different discipline, the real exercise of arms. You must not contend one with another in sport; but must venture to face an enemy, where there is such a thing as danger. You must give over your dust and your oil, and teach your young men the use of the bow and the javelin, not putting into their hands such light things as a puff of wind would blow away; let them have

a sturdy

a fturdy lance that whizzes through the air, a
swinging great stone, a sword, a shield, a breast-
plate, a helmet. As matters are managed at
present, you must have been protected by the
kindness of some good-natured divinity; or half
a handful of light-armed soldiers would have
done your business before now. If I should
draw this dagger from my belt, and singly attack your army of heroes, I warrant I should
soon make an end of their sport. I should be
master of the field, while every one would fly
helterskelter, not being able to endure the sight
of a naked sword. I should laugh heartily to
see them with tears in their eyes, and their knees
knocking together, creeping for shelter behind
statues and pillars. They would not then look
so ruddy, but would have the paleness of
ashes, the tint which fear bestows. Indeed
such has been the effect of a profound peace,
that I question whether you could bear to behold the crest of an adverse helmet.

SOLON.

Nobody ever gave this account of us before;
neither the Thracians who made war upon us
under

under the command of Eumolpus, nor your Amazons with Hippolyta at their head, nor any who spoke from experience. For, my good Sir, though our young men are naked when they perform their exercise, we do not therefore expose them unarmed to the dangers of war: but, when they are perfect in these games, we then put arms into their hands, which they manage so much the better for having been thus prepared.

ANACHARSIS.

And where is this military school of yours? I have seen nothing like it, though I have been all over the city.

SOLON.

If you stay any considerable time longer amongst us, you will see that each of us has a variety of arms, to be used on occasion. We have helmets, and horses, and caparisons. About one fourth part of our whole number are horsemen. But in peace we can see no necessity for being always armed, and never being seen without an instrument of death. Accordingly any

man

man who wears a sword in the city, or goes
armed in publick without cause, is liable to a
penalty. You Scythians indeed are very ex-
cusable, if you go armed all your lives. For,
being without fortifications, you are not only
expofed to continual furprifes and incursions,
but are always in a state of warfare. For you
can never be certain, that somebody or other
will not fall upon you, while you are sleeping
in your waggon, and drag you out, and kill
you. That mutual distrust, which must be in
a society not restrained by laws, where all men
live as they list, makes a sword always necessary; for no one can tell how soon he may be
attacked.

ANACHARSIS.

So, Sir, you think it idle to wear a sword
without absolute necessity, and spare your arms,
for fear of wearing them out with handling;
laying them up against the time when they must
be used. But you do not argue in this manner
with regard to your young men. Without any
sufficient reason you waste them with toil, you
batter them with needless blows, you roll them
in

in dust and dirt, you dissolve them in sweat, to answer no purpose at all.

SOLON.

You seem, Anacharsis, to entertain the same notion of bodily strength, as of wine, or water. You think it will evaporate by labour, as liquor does out of a jar, and leave nothing behind but a body empty and dry. But this is so far from being the case, that the more you draw off your strength in exercise, the faster it flows in; not unlike the Hydra in the Fable, which, as fast as one head was cut off, had two sprung up in its room. Indeed the feeble body, that has not been used to exercise, and has not substance to withstand fatigue, may well be injured and wasted by labour: since the very same blast, that mends the fire, would infallibly blow out the candle.

ANACHARSIS.

I do not very well understand what you say: it requires a more close attention, as well as a more acute discernment than I am master of. But I would gladly know the reason, that, neither

ther in the Olympian, nor Pythian, nor Isthmian, nor other games, resorted to by such a vast concourse of spectators, you exhibit no contest in arms; but only expose your naked champions to be kicked and beaten, rewarding the victorious with apples and olive boughs. This is very particular, and requires explanation.

SOLON.

We think, Anacharsis, that this method of proceeding will make our young men much more eager and fond of exercise, when they see those who excel thus honoured, and their merits proclaimed before all Greece. Knowing before whom they are to appear undressed, they naturally provide the best stock of health and strength, with whatever can make them worthy of victory, and save them from shame. And then our rewards, as I said before, are not inconsiderable: to be applauded by all the spectators, to be the most distinguished, to be pointed out as excelling all competitors, are prizes worth contending for. Hence it is that many of the spectators, who are of an age not unfit for those exercises, depart from the place inflamed

flamed with the love of virtue and labour. This
is of such consequence, O Anacharsis, that, were
the love of glory banished from the world, I
know not what good would be left in it, nor
where we should find any effectual motive to a
memorable action. From their great eagerness
in contending naked for an apple, or a wreath
of wild olive, you may imagine how they will
behave with arms in their hands, fighting for
the defence of their country, their religion,
their wives and children. I wonder what you
would say, if you were to behold the battles of
our quails and [b] fighting cocks, and our great
fondness for such fights. You would surely
laugh, especially when you hear that all is according
to law, and that our young men are
obliged to be present, and behold these birds
fight to the last extremity. Neither is this so ridiculous
as you may imagine. By impercepti-

[b] Themistocles, having observed, that cocks are always
ready to fight without any reason, recommended them to his
army, as heroes well worthy of imitation. Of which having
found the good effects, the Athenians, ever intent on improving
the morals of their country, established cock-fighting
by law. Ælian, V. H. ii. c. 28. Perhaps every admirer of
that elegant amusement may not have read Ælian.

ble degrees a contempt of danger takes possession of the soul. No one would be thought to have less spirit and courage than a game-cock; and no one is unwilling to encounter wounds, labours, and difficulties. As to making trial of our youth in arms, and exposing them to be wounded by one another, that would be acting the part of savages to all intents and purposes. Besides, that it would be foolish to throw away in sport the lives of our best men, who may be so much better employed against our enemies. You talk, Anacharsis, of visiting the other parts of Greece. Pray remember, when you come to Sparta, not to laugh, nor think it labour in vain, when you see them beating one another about the theatre for a ball. The followers of Lycurgus and those of Hercules go into a place surrounded with water, where, being stripped and drawn up like two armies, they fall upon each other and fight, till one or the other party is driven either out of the inclosure, or into the water. After which hostilities cease, and peace ensues. What will you think, when you see them whipped at the altar, till they stream with blood; while
their

their fathers and mothers look on without the least symptom of any other concern than lest they should shrink; threatening, begging, and beseeching them to bear their flogging as long as possible? Many have died of the stripes thus given them, scorning to survive the shame of yielding to the lash in the presence of their relations. You will see statues erected to their honour at the publick expence. Take care you entertain no suspicions of their being mad, nor make any observations on their causing unnecessary pain, when neither domestick tyrant nor foreign enemy gives them any occasion. I dare say that Lycurgus, their lawgiver, could have alledged many plausible arguments in defence of his institution. He would have made it appear, that, being their friend, he could not intend any hostile oppression, nor out of ill-will thus to waste the rising strength of the state; but that his design was, to make those, who were to defend their country, superior to every pain. And you may very well imagine, without consulting Lycurgus, that such a Spartan, when taken prisoner in war, and put to the torture, will not suffer one improper word

to

to escape him. He smiles at his tormentors, and, with invincible fortitude of mind, makes it difficult to judge, whether what he undergoes will first tire his enemy or himself.

ANACHARSIS.

Pray, Sir, was Lycurgus himself whipped in his youthful days? or did he produce this pretty invention of his at an age when he was too old to partake of the amusement?

SOLON.

He made these laws when he was an old man, after his return from Crete. He had gone to reside some time amongst the Cretans, to have an opportunity of learning their excellent laws, of which Minos the son of Jupiter was the author.

ANACHARSIS.

I am amazed, Solon, that you do not imitate Lycurgus in this beating of the poor boys; which is so fine a thing, and so worthy of you.

SOLON.

The reason is, our own country exercises are sufficient for our purpose, and we are not fond of copying foreign fashions.

ANA-

ANACHARSIS.

That is not the thing. You cannot but be sensible of the absurdity of scourging a poor naked object with his hands above his head, for no earthly advantage publick or private. If I should travel to Sparta, and be there during the solemnity of such proceedings, I must expect to be overwhelmed with a shower of stones. For who could forbear affronting a people, that whip their innocent children, like so many thieves or pickpockets? Really in my mind the city, that can suffer such ridiculous customs, wants to be well purged with hellebore.

SOLON.

Do not think, Sir, that you have carried your cause, because there is nobody here to contradict you. You will find that the Spartans can defend their own customs.—But now that I have finished my account of our exercises, which you seem not very highly to relish, I hope you will indulge me in turn with an account of your manner of training up your
young

young men in Scythia, what exercises you have, and how you make them honest and brave.

ANACHARSIS.

It is but fair, Solon. I will certainly give you an account of our Scythian customs, which are not so respectable as to resemble yours. For we are such cowards, that we cannot bear a single flap on the face—but, if you please, we will defer it till to-morrow, that I may consider more at leisure what I have heard, and bethink myself better of what I am to say. Let us go; for it is almost night.

ON POETICAL INSPIRATION.

LYCINUS

AND

HESIOD.

U,

ON POETICAL INSPIRATION.

LYCINUS.

THAT you are an admirable poet, and that your verses as well as your laurel were given you by the Muses, no man can doubt; since we have your own [*i*] word for it in those sublime and celestial poems. Yet that preface of yours might pose one, where you talk of having been gifted with the precious faculty of verse-making, that you might celebrate things past, and foretel things to come. The one of these indeed you have fully executed, going through the whole genealogy of the gods, as far back as Chaos, Earth, Heaven, and Love. You have sung the praises of women, and the

[*i*] Hef. Theog. xxx.

pre-

precepts of agriculture. Besides a multitude
of other things, you have let us into the secrets
of the seven stars, have taught plowing and
reaping, and told us the best time to set sail.
This part of your undertaking you have performed
to a tittle. But as to the foretelling of
future events, which would have been beyond
comparison more for the emolument of mankind,
and much more like the munificent gods,
concerning that you have been quite silent;
you have not even made the least attempt,
leaving things entirely in the dark: so that
your poetry in that respect has nothing of the
merit of Calchas, Telephus, Polyidus, or Phineus.
These men never pretended to the good
graces of the Muses; yet they foretold abundance
of events, and disdained not to clear up
the doubts of their humble supplicants. So
that one of these three charges you cannot but
admit. Either you told a lie, (begging your
pardon) when you said the Muses had promised
you the power of divination. Or, if they really
did bestow that faculty on you, you have
invidiously concealed it, nor been of the least
use to those who stand in need of it. Or else
perhaps

perhaps you have written several poems on the subject, of which for some unknown reason you reserve the publication to a future time. For I would not undertake to say, that the Muses, after their double promise, have granted one half, and withheld the other. Especially as the knowledge of future events was the first part of their inspired declaration. However you are certainly the properest man to be consulted in what relates to yourself. For it can never be disagreeable to the gods, who so generously bestow what they have, for you their friends and disciples to dispel our doubts, and tell us the whole truth of what you know.

HESIOD.

It would be very easy, Sir, to stop your mouth, by observing to you, that nothing in my poems is to be placed to my account, but to that of the Muses. Your way therefore would be, to go to the fountain-head, and demand of them their reasons for saying and not saying certain things. As to what proceeded more immediately from my own stock of knowledge, which pertains to the driving, feeding, milking, and management of cattle, I am ready, as it becomes me, to give the best account I can of it. But the Muses give no other reason than their own will and pleasure for bestowing their favours on whom and to what degree they think fit. However you shall not complain of a poet's want of apology. Though I cannot allow that our works ought to have their every syllable sifted with such perfect minuteness. If, in the heat of his career, something escape the poet's judgment, you should not be over-rigid to examine; but consider, that, for the sake of measure and harmony in our numbers, we are forced to say many things, which we do not entirely mean. There are certain modes of expression, which we cannot avoid giving into, to keep up the smoothness of versification. But you would wantonly rob us of what we poets prize above all, the flights of fancy, and the indulgence of our invention. You wilfully pass over the numberless beauties of our compositions, and cavil for ever at exceptions, delighted with finding fault. But you are not the only carping critick, nor I the only bard abused. My brother Homer has fallen

into

into the hands of not a few induſtrious to diſ-
cover blemiſhes in his admirable poems. But,
if it be neceſſary to wave theſe general remarks,
and come more particularly to the point, I
ſhall only beg the favour of you, good Sir,
to read over my Works and Days. In that
poem you cannot fail to find abundant tokens
of the divine prophetick muſe, foretelling the
ſucceſs of ſeaſonable labours, and pointing out
the future puniſhment of negligence.

[k] Untimely tillage ſcarce thy baſket fills.

I have ſhewn at large the proſperous events that
ſkilful huſbandmen may fairly expect; which
certainly is a kind of divination the moſt uſe-
ful of any.

LYCINUS.

Indeed, dread Sir, this ſilly manner of de-
fending yourſelf looks as if it really was ſome
goddeſs who gave you your verſes. But, as to
ſuch predictions as you mention, we could
have made them ourſelves, without the help
of either you or your Muſes. When poets and
pierians fall a propheſying, they ſhould propheſy

[k] Heſiod's Works and Days, il. ver. 160.

like themselves. But there is not a farmer living, who cannot tell that plenty of rain will produce a plentiful crop, and that, when the fields are burnt up with long drought, there will infallibly be a scarcity. Every one knows, that the middle of summer is not the season for plowing, and that sowing requires care; that corn is not to be reaped whilst it is green, because it then contains nothing of use. We can guess too without a prophet, that the seed should be well harrowed in, to save it from the crows. These rules are founded on reason, and are undoubtedly very just. But then they are not to be considered as any branch of the prophetick art, which is employed in discovering what is obscure, and beyond the reach of mere man. For instance, to foretel to Minos, that his son would be choaked in a tub of honey [*l*], to explain the cause of Apollo's anger, and predict the ten years siege of Troy; there was prophecy, if you please. But, if what you mention is to be deemed such, then I too am a prophet, as well as you. Without one drop of Castalian dew, without either lau-

[*l*] Hom. Il. i. ver. 93. and ii. ver. 300 to 332.

rel

rel or Delphick tripod, I will undertake to say, that, if a man goes out naked in the sharp air amidst rain or hail, he will assuredly be seized with a cold fit of an ague; and, what is more wonderful still, a hot fit will succeed: besides a multitude of other things, which it would be idle to mention. But, if you will be ruled by me, drop such silly pretensions, and stick to what you first set out with. Say that your verses were not of your own production, but that you wrote under the influence of something divine; which was however not entirely to be relied on, since it made good one half of its promise, and neglected the other half.

THE

The COUNCIL of the Gods [m].

JUPITER, MERCURY, and MOMUS.

[b] This council of the gods is in the style and manner of the Athenian assemblies. The several offices of Jupiter, Neptune, Apollo, &c. mentioned in the preamble of the decree, could not be exactly rendered into English in so many words. Whoever would know more of the nature of an assembly at Athens, may take the pains to read the ΕΚΚΛΗΣΙΑΣΟΥΣΑΙ of Aristophanes.

The COUNCIL of the GODS.

JUPITER.

FOR the future, ye gods, let me have none of your whispering, running into corners, laying your heads together, and muttering against several that you think ought to be kicked out of the company: but, since a council has been summoned, let every one declare his sentiments openly and above-board, blaming whatever is blame-worthy. Do you, Mercury, make proclamation according to law.

MERCURY.

All manner of persons are hereby commanded to keep silence! If any of the old established gods chooses to speak to the question concerning upstarts and intruders, let him come forth, and he shall be heard!

MOMUS.

MOMUS.

I shall offer a few words, Jupiter, with your leave.

JUPITER.

Pr'ythee do not ask any more leave: you are allowed to speak by proclamation.

MOMUS.

I say then, that I think some here are very much in the wrong, who, of men being made gods, are not contented to have the privilege to themselves; but nothing less will serve their turn than admitting pages and attendants to the same honour. I beg, Jupiter, that I may not be under any restraint; for that would prevent my speaking at all. And every body knows how free I am of my tongue, and how unwilling to keep it still, when any thing is amiss. I am used to scrutinize every action openly, and speak my mind without favour or affection, without fear or dread. For which reason most people consider me as a very troublesome fellow, and call me the common informer. However, since it is allowed by law,
and

and by proclamation, and by you, Jupiter, I will freely speak my mind without reserve. I say then, that there are many, who, not satisfied with being admitted themselves into our society and to a share of our good living, though but half divine: have notwithstanding introduced into Heaven their servants and associate revellers, and had them enrolled in the number of gods; so that they partake of the sacrifices, and have an equal share of the good cheer; though not one of them has paid for being made free of the company.

JUPITER.

Do not you go about the bush, Momus; but speak out plainly and distinctly, and name names. You have expressed yourself in such a manner, as to raise various suspicions amongst us one of another; which is enough to set us all together by the ears. But a free speaker should not scruple to declare himself in the most particular manner.

MOMUS.

I am heartily glad, Jupiter, that you are for plainness of speech. That is greatly and
royally

royally said. So have amongst you! For I will not spare your names. In the first place then, there is that good gentleman Bacchus, so far from being a complete god, that he is but half a Greek; the grandson of one Cadmus, a Phœnician vagabond. What a life he has led since his coming among us, I need not mention; as every body must have observed his foppish bonnet, his drunkenness, and his gait. No one can be ignorant what a dissolute mad being he is, never sober from the moment he wakes! Yet this fellow has brought amongst us his whole fraternity, his whole band of buffoons, Pan, Silenus, and the Satyrs; a number of monstrous, ugly, dancing, goatish boars! Pan has horns, being half a goat, which he very much resembles in the length of his beard. Silenus is a flat-nosed, bald-pated old fellow, a Lydian by nation, who generally rides upon an ass. The Satyrs have sharp-pointed ears, are bald, and have little horns like those of a kid. These last are Phrygians. They have all of them tails. And is not this elegant society? No wonder mortals laugh at such respectable divinities! I do not mention the two women.

He

He has placed the crown of his mistress Ariadne amongst the constellations; nor has he neglected the daughter of Icarius, the [*n*] ploughman. But, what is best of all, he has also introduced into Heaven Erigone's lap-dog, lest the poor girl should grow melancholy for the loss of her companion. Are not these very pretty doings? You allow all this, I hope, to be scandalous, mad, and ridiculous. But you shall hear more.

JUPITER.

I see which way the game is going. But not a word about Æsculapius or Hercules, I beseech you. The former is a physician [*o*], one worth many; and my son Hercules, I am sure, has dearly bought his immortality. So not a syllable against them! do you hear?

MOMUS.

For your sake, Jupiter, I forbear; though I could say a word or two. To be sure they

[*n*] This ploughman first taught the use of wine. The reader will determine, whether he was worth mentioning in a note.
[*o*] Hom. Il. xi. ver. 514.

do still retain the marks of the [p] fire; but that is neither here nor there.—I wish I might once be permitted to speak of Jupiter himself.

JUPITER.

You are permitted. You do not pretend to make an alien of me?

MOMUS.

They say something like it in Crete, where there is a sepulchre which they shew, calling it Jupiter's. But I believe them as little as I do the Ægienses, who insist upon it, that you are not of the true breed. I shall only take the liberty of observing a few things in you, that are not quite so becoming. You yourself were the first promoter of these disorders. You have filled our assembly with bastards, visiting the strumpets of mortality in all manner of shapes. We have sometimes been in dreadful apprehensions, lest some pious votary should lay hold of you in the disguise of a bull, and sacrifice you to Jupiter. When you assumed the appearance of gold, we were afraid of your fal-

---

[p] Æsculapius was knocked down by a thunderbolt, and Hercules died on a funeral pile.

ling into a crucible; after which all that remained of the mighty Jove might have been worn as a necklace, a bracelet, or an ear-ring. Indeed it is a great shame, I must needs say, for you thus to fill Heaven with demigods. What must any one think to hear of Hercules being deified? while Eurystheus, who set him to work, is dead and buried! Near to the temple of Hercules the servant, is the grave of Eurystheus his master! Then again at Thebes Bacchus is made a god! while his cousins Pentheus, Actæon, and Learchus, are the veriest wretches of all mortal men. But truly, since you set the fashion of loving flesh and blood, all the rest do the same: not only the gods, the filthy he-creatures, but the delicate goddesses too must copy their righteous pattern. All the world have heard of other intrigues besides those of Anchises, [*q*] Tithonus, Endymion, and Jasiones [*r*].

JUPITER.

Pry'thee, Momús, say nothing about Ganymede. I shall take it very ill, if you up-

[*q*] Virg. Æn. iv. 585.
[*r*] Hom. Odyss. v. 125.

braid him with his family, and make the poor boy fret.

MOMUS.

I suppose too that I am to make no mention of the eagle, which has been advanced into heaven, is perched upon the imperial sceptre, and goes near to nestle on thy awful head, in all the pomp of divinity! But we must be silent on this subject also, for the sake of Ganymede. But pray tell me, Jupiter, whence came Attis, and Corybas, and Sabazius? Then there is Mithres, the Mede; he neither dresses nor speaks like a Greek. I do not think he would understand you, if you were to drink to him. The Scythians and Getæ, seeing this method of proceeding, have fairly given your supremacy the slip, and make their gods among themselves, just as they like; by which means Zamolxis the slave has been deified, sneaking in amongst us I know not how. All this however, ye gods, is still tolerable. But who art thou, O Egyptian [1] dog's face, adorned with this

[1] See the Abbé Pluche's Histoire du Ciel. The common account is, that the rebellion of the giants occasioned the gods to quit their habitations in a fright, and fly into Ægypt, where they made beasts of themselves.

fine

fine linen? will thy barking prove thee a god? And what has that spotted Memphian bull to do with oracles and priests? I am ashamed to mention the ibis, the ape, the goat, and other divinities still more ridiculous, which have got out of Ægypt, and are so strangely stuffed into Heaven. How can ye bear, ye gods, to see such intruders put upon an equal footing with, nay honoured more than, yourselves? Pray, Jupiter, how do you like the ram's horns on your head?

JUPITER.

You tell strange stories of the Ægyptians, I confess. But they contain mysteries, not to be ridiculed by the profane.

MOMUS.

One has need of mysteries, to be sure, to discern that gods are gods, and dogs faces dogs faces!

JUPITER.

Say no more about the Ægyptians at present. We will settle that affair another time, when we have leisure. Now proceed to the rest.

MOMUS.

MOMUS.

There is Trophonius, and (what is more provoking) there is Amphilochus, who, being the son of an abominable matricide, utters oracles in Cilicia, deals in a thousand lies, and sells witchcraft in small quantities. So that Apollo is out of repute. Every stone, and every altar, is now an oracle, provided it be sprinkled with oil, and crowned with garlands, and attended by a juggler, which last may be had any where. The statue of Polydamas the wrestler cures fevers in Olympia, as that of Theagenes does in Thasus. Hector is treated with sacrifices in Ilium, and Protesilaus over-against him in Chersonesus. And, now that we are so scandalously multiplied, perjury and sacrilege have increased in proportion; and all reasonable beings hold us in contempt. So much for bastards and impostors. But when I hear many strange names of things which are not here, and cannot be any where else, I am ready to burst. Where is this celebrated *Virtue*, and *Nature*, and *Fate*, and *Fortune*, to be found? a pack of idle names invented

vented by a set of blockheads, who call themselves philosophers! which though no more than fictions to serve a turn, yet so effectually have they perverted the minds of weak people, that no man living thinks any longer of sacrificing to us; being fully persuaded, that millions of hecatombs offered to us would signify nothing, and that Fortune will infallibly bring about whatever the Fates have originally decreed. I should be glad to know, Jupiter, if ever you saw any such persons as *Virtue*, or *Nature*, or *Fate*; which you must so often have heard of, unless you are so deaf, that you cannot even hear the clamours of philosophy? I had a great deal more to say; but I will conclude. For I see I have sweated a good many here, who would be glad to silence my enquiries with a hiss. For a conclusion therefore, if you like it, Jupiter, I will read you a decree, which I have drawn up concerning them.

JUPITER.

Read it. I find there are many things, which require being looked into, and the sooner the better.

THE

THE DECREE.

"May Fortune favour!"

A council being called according to law, on the seventh day of this month, Jupiter presided, assisted by Apollo and Neptune; Momus was nocturnal secretary, and the god of sleep recited.

Forasmuch as many strangers, not only Greeks, but Barbarians, by no means fit company for us, have, I know not how, obtained the name of gods, and, being enrolled of our order, have filled up the seats of Heaven; so that our good fellowship is disturbed by the noise, riot, and gibberish of the scum of the earth; so that ambrosia begins to fail, and nectar is already raised to a [r] mina the half-pint, on account of the great demand: and whereas they have had the impudence to push the true veteran gods out of their places, and seat themselves before them, contrary to all rule and order, and venture to arrogate to themselves the highest honours from mortals on earth; May it please the senate and people, that an as-

[r] 3*l*. 4*s*. 7*d*.

sembly

sembly be held in Olympus about the winter solstice, and seven genuine gods be chosen to take cognizance of the affair, three of the ancient council of Saturn, and four of the twelve, Jupiter being one; who, before they sit in judgment, shall solemnly swear by Styx, as the law requires. After which, let Mercury make proclamation, and bring before them all who demand a place here, provided with responsible witnesses, and certificates of their family. Then let them be heard one after another; and the judges, having carefully enquired into their several pretensions, will either publickly pronounce them gods, or send them down to their graves, to lodge with their ancestors. And, if any one thus disproved and rejected by the judges, shall be caught afterwards intruding into heaven, let him be tossed immediately to hell head foremost. And, for the future, let every one mind his own business. Let not Minerva be dabbling in physick, nor Æsculapius pretend to prophesy. Apollo is not to meddle with so many things at once; but must resolve on sticking entirely to either his fortune-telling, his harp, or his quackery. As for the philosophers,

sophers, let them be forbidden any longer to invent new-fangled names, or pretend to talk of what they know nothing about. Whoever has unfairly obtained a temple, and been divinely honoured on false pretences, let his statue be pulled down, and that of Jupiter, or Juno, or Apollo, or some other, be set up in the place. For such deceivers let the city provide a sepulchre, and give them a grave-stone instead of an altar. Whoever shall disregard the proclamation, and refuse to take his trial, let him be condemned unheard. Such is the decree.

JUPITER.

And it is most just. Let every one, who approves of it, hold up his hand! or rather let it be ratified without farther ceremony! For I know a great many will have no stomach to it. Now you may go for the present. But when Mercury shall summon you, take care to come, and bring every one his proper testimonials, setting forth the name of his father and mother, as well as his tribe and fraternity,
where

where he was born, and why he was made a god. Whoever shall not thus appear, and answer for himself in a satisfactory manner, will no longer be thought any thing in heaven, though he have a superb temple on earth, and be there deemed a mighty divinity.

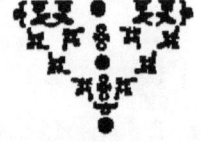

THE

THE CYNICK [*].

[*] St. Chrysostom is said to have converted this dialogue into a homily.

The CYNICK and LYCINUS.

LYCINUS.

IN the name of wonder, why this appearance? Long hair, an enormous beard, but not one inch of coat [*p*]! almoſt naked, no ſhoes! Upon my word, Sir, you ſeem to be a ſort of ſtrolling bear, except that you are ſo cruel to your own body. You are never out of your way, I fancy. The hard ground does vēry well for a bed. But really you uſe that old cloak ſcandalouſly, in expoſing it ſo to all the dirt and naſtineſs you can pick up. Though, I muſt confeſs, it is none of the fineſt, and in its beſt ſtate could make no very flaſhy appearance.

[*p*] Γυμνοδρμῆ here can only mean, that the ſkin appeared through certain apertures in the dreſs. A man quite naked would hardly be reproached with his rags.

Y   CYNICK.

CYNICK.

I should be sorry, if it did. Whatever is easiest to be got, and gives least trouble when one has it, is the thing for me. Pray do not you look upon luxury as a vice?

LYCINUS.

Certainly.

CYNICK.

And is not frugality a virtue?

LYCINUS.

Surely.

CYNICK.

How comes it then, that you pretend to find fault with my simplicity, and pass over other mens extravagance?

LYCINUS.

Simplicity do you call it? To me it appears the last degree of comfortless poverty! For you live no better than the beggar, who seeks his daily bread from door to door.

CYNICK.

CYNICK.

Since you go to that, suppose we fairly discuss what is poverty, and what is not?

LYCINUS.

With all my heart.

CYNICK.

Will you allow that to be a sufficiency, which extends to the whole of a man's wants?

LYCINUS.

Yes.

CYNICK.

And is not that poverty, which falls short of a man's wants?

LYCINUS.

Yes.

CYNICK.

But that is by no means the case with me, for I have not one necessary unsupplied.

LYCINUS.

How can that be?

CYNICK.

Very well. As you will allow, if you only consider to what end every thing wanted is designed; as, for example, that a house is intended to shelter us.

LYCINUS.

Well.

CYNICK.

And a garment, is not that too for shelter?

LYCINUS.

Yes.

CYNICK.

And pray to what purpose does a man require shelter? is it not for the good of what is sheltered?

LYCINUS.

Truly I think so.

CYNICK.

CYNICK.

Do you think my feet the worſe for want of it?

LYCINUS.

I cannot tell.

CYNICK.

But you may ſoon know. What is the office of feet?

LYCINUS.

Walking.

CYNICK.

And do not you think, that my feet are as fit for that purpoſe as thoſe of another?

LYCINUS.

Poſſibly they may.

CYNICK.

Well, let them be better or worſe, do not you think they perform their office?

LYCINUS.

Perhaps they may.

CYNICK.

CYNICK.

If they do that, my feet are as good as another's.

LYCINUS.

Well.

CYNICK.

Then what do you say to my body? am I worse provided than others in that respect? If my body were a bad one, it would be a weak one. For the perfection of the body consists in strength. Is mine weak?

LYCINUS.

I cannot say that it seems so.

CYNICK.

Neither my feet, nor any part of my body is in want of covering. If so, I should feel it. For any want unsatisfied creates a degree of wretchedness. But my body does not appear to want any nourishment, though it be supported in this accidental manner, by whatever falls in my way.

LYCI-

LYCINUS.

I do not see that it does.

CYNICK.

If I were badly fed, I should not be so strong; for bad victuals impair the body.

LYCINUS.

True.

CYNICK.

How then, I pray, can you talk at the rate you have done, degrading me, and undervaluing my way of living?

LYCINUS.

Because, notwithstanding that your adored Nature and the gods have set this world before us, and have been such generous providers, that not only our necessities, but our pleasures have been consulted; yet you are utterly thrown out of your share of most things, and partake of little more than a beast does. For you drink water, as a beast does; you make a meal of whatever you find, as a dog does; you sleep

upon the ground, as a dog does. You have
a cloak indeed, but it is such as a beggar would
hardly stoop to pick up. If there be wisdom
in being contented with such a condition as
yours, I am sure there was no wisdom in the
gods, when they provided us sheep, and wool,
and oil, and honey, and a profusion of good
wine, besides the infinite variety of other things;
in giving us eatables of every kind, in regaling
us with such excellent liquor, in furnishing
our pockets with money and our beds with
down, in bestowing upon us fine houses, and
wonderfully preventing almost every wish. Our
elegancies are indeed the immediate effect of
human art: but it is from heaven that we have
that art. Now it is a most wretched thing to
be deprived of the comforts of life by another
man, as a prisoner is. But to deprive one's
self of them, is downright madness, and nothing
else.

CYNICK.

You reason well. But hear me. If, when
a great man gives a sumptuous treat to a vast
number of guests of all kinds, any one of them
should

should take it into his head to seize and devour whatever he can lay his hands on, making a jumble the most fatal to his constitution, and should take as much pains to cram one belly as would be sufficient for twenty; pray what would you say of such a man? you could not call him considerate.

LYCINUS.

No, to be sure.

CYNICK.

Does he act wisely?

LYCINUS.

No.

CYNICK.

But the guest, who, not tempted with the vast variety of dishes, decently eats a moderate quantity of the one thing next to him, without a wishful eye to the rest, is certainly a wiser and better man than the other.

LYCINUS.

Certainly.

CYNICK.

CYNICK.

Do you guess what I am bringing out? or must I be more explicit?

LYCINUS.

Explain, pr'ythee.

CYNICK.

The gods are those munificent hosts, who provide all things of every kind in the greatest plenty; that every man, let him be sick or well, strong or weak, may have what is suitable to him: and not that all men should have all things at once, but only what is best adapted to the particular case of each. You are the rapacious guest, who, never being satisfied, would have all the provisions to himself. You claim every thing as your property, in the sea, on the land, in the air. Not contented with the pleasures that may be had at home, you import from the remotest corners of the world the materials of luxury; always preferring foreign to domestick enjoyments, expence to moderation, things got with difficulty to things
procured

procured with ease; in short, always preferring hurry and vexation to quiet and content. It is by much misery and sorrow, that you obtain these precious blessed abundant privileges. Gold and silver so desirable, fine houses, fine clothes and furniture, and all their costly consequences, with what trouble and fatigue, what danger, what blood, slaughter, and destruction, are they procured! For the sake of your dear money how many lives are lost at sea! how many evils attend the pursuit! what animosities, quarrels, and assassinations, does it produce! friend is opposed to friend, the son to the father, the wife to her husband! for gold [*u*] Eriphyle betrayed her husband! And yet whoever found any extraordinary warmth in an embroidered coat? does the gilded cieling make the house more secure? does the silver cup improve the liquor? does the golden or ivory bedstead render sleep the sweeter? I fancy you may often find the blessed incumbent restless on down, sleepless in a bed of state. And all the trouble-

[*u*]   Concidit auguris
  Argivi domus, ob lucrum
      Demersa exitio.   Hor. lib. iii. Ode 16.

some variety, the expensive elegance of eating, does but destroy the strength, and engender diseases. It would be endless to enumerate the pains and plagues of love, arising from the excess of a passion, which might easily be regulated, if the rage of luxury were restrained. All this madness falls short of the present system of manners. The natural use of things in general is as much perverted, as when a bed is turned into a chariot.

LYCINUS.

Who does that?

CYNICK.

You, who use men as beasts of burden. You loll at your ease in your litters on their shoulders. You drive them this way or that way, like asses: and in this consists your felicity. There is a certain fish, which you are not contented to use merely for food, as nature intended; but you make a purple die of it.

LYCINUS.

Surely there is no perversion of nature in that, since it is fit for both purposes.

CYNICK.

CYNICK.

Nature never meant it for a die. You might possibly use a cup as a jar; but it was not made for that. But there is no such thing as reckoning up one half of the calamities which men bring upon themselves. And yet you blame me for avoiding them. I, like the moderate man at the feast, am satisfied with what my situation offers; I aim at no variety nor abundance dearly bought, but enjoy what is easily obtained. Since therefore my wants are few, and my desires soon satisfied, you think I live like a beast! at this rate what will you say of the gods, who have no wants at all? But the better to comprehend the distinction between having many wants and few, be pleased to consider, that the less perfect your condition is, the more are your wants: children have more wants than grown persons, women than men, sick than well. The gods, being perfect, want nothing; and, the nearer any one approaches to the divine nature, the fewer his wants. Can you suppose that [w] Hercules, that divine

[w] Hercules was the favourite god of the Cynicks. " He

divine man, who roamed over the world with no other dress than a lion's skin—can you suppose that he wandered in misery and want? Could he be miserable, who removed the misery of others; or poor, who was master by sea and land? Whatever he undertook he always accomplished; nor did he ever find his equal, much less his superior, while he remained in the number of men. You do not imagine, that it was for want of shoes to his feet, or clothes to his back, that so distinguished a man wandered about the world. It was because he was temperate and brave, and loved conquest, and contemned luxury. What do you think of Theseus, his disciple? was he not king of all the Athenians, the son of Neptune, as they say, and the greatest hero of his age? Yet it was his choice to go naked and barefooted, and to cherish the hairs on his head and beard, as was the general taste of antiquity. For our ancestors were not like their degenerate sons, and

"He was pointed out by the ancient Heathens, as their great exemplar of virtue. The idea of virtue with them consisted chiefly in seeking and undergoing fatigues with steadiness and patience." Polymetis, p. 114.

would

would as soon have followed the present fashion, as a lion would submit to be shaved. Softness and smoothness and delicacy of skin, in their opinion, best became women: they, who were men, chose to appear so, and regarded their beard as their honour, which nature as much intended to be the distinguishing ornament of a man, as a mane to adorn a horse, or his shaggy chin the lion. Those ancients would I emulate, those ancients I long to equal! But truly I have no stomach for the splendid misery of the moderns; nor do I envy them their costly tables, or their fine clothes. Indeed they take wonderful pains to polish and smooth the whole body, not suffering even the most hidden part to escape as simple nature intended it! For my part, I should not be sorry to have feet like those of a horse, as, they say, Chiron had. I wish to want covering as little as a lion does; and to live on cheap food, as the happy dogs do. May a clod of earth suffice for my pillow! may I consider the whole world as my home! may my sustenance be such as falls in my way! as to gold and silver, may neither I nor any of my friends ever desire them, the infernal cause

cause of every evil, the constant source of
sedition, war, treachery, and slaughter! may I
learn to wish for no more than enough; and,
if I have less, let me bear it patiently! Such
are my sentiments, very different from those of
the vulgar. It is not therefore at all to be
wondered at, that my appearance and manner
of life should be so very different, when my
purposes are so. I am amazed how you can
ever conceive it right, for a harper, or a piper,
or a player, to be distinguished by his dress;
but that the figure and garb of a man of virtue
should be precisely the same with that of the
rascally multitude. But, if the good are to be
distinguished by a peculiar habit, what can become them more than this of mine, which is
so directly the reverse of foppery? To be rough
and dirty, to wear a ragged cloak, to let my
hair grow its own way, and to go without
shoes, is my habit. Yours resembles that of
an infamous prostitute to unnatural passion;
and I defy any of them to go beyond you in
the modish colour, the tawdry finery, the variety of your habiliments, the spruceness of your
shoes, or the preparation and adjustment of
your

your perfumed hair. Your similarity of scent
serves to class you with those vile wretches.
And is this worthy of any thing called man?
You are as little fit for the enduring of labour
as they are, and as much abandoned to pleasure.
You eat as delicately as they; you sleep, you
walk, in the same manner. Nay, you scarcely
condescend to walk at all, but must be carried, like so many knapsacks, some by cattle,
and others by men. My feet are sufficient to
convey me whithersoever I think proper. I
bear the heat and cold with unconcern, nor ever
make my condition worse than it is, by mur-
muring at providence. You, who are so happy forsooth, are never satisfied, but always finding fault. You are always impatient of your
present circumstances, which you perpetually
desire to change. In winter you long for summer, and in summer for winter. When the
weather is cold, you wish it hot; and, when it
is hot, you wish it cold. You are never pleased,
but always peevish and complaining. You are
splenetick, and sick of a surfeit. [a] What is
the

[a] Something like this seems intended by the original
passage, which Joannes Jensius has had the courage to own
himself.

the most extraordinary is, that, being the wretches you are, whose whole lives are governed by fashion and folly, you are constantly endeavouring to make others as miserable as yourselves. You are not unlike those borne down by a torrent: they go with the stream, and you are hurried on by your passions. A certain man, having mounted a mad horse, found himself unable either to stop him, or to alight. Somebody chanced to meet him, and asked, whither he was going. "Just whither he thinks proper," answered he, nodding his head at the horse. If one should put the same question to you, you must, if you speak truth, answer in general, that you go whithersoever your passions happen to hurry you. Or, to be particular, you must say, your pleasure, your ambition, your avarice, your anger, your fear, or some other substantial motive of the same kind. For, not contented with one, you ride many mad horses by turns; while this carries you one way, and that another. You gallop furiously into pits

---

himself puzzled with. "Where you are ignorant, you should confess you are ignorant," said Swift to Sheridan, vol. xii. p. 131.

and

and over precipices; and never dream of a fall, till you are fairly down. But this old tattered cloak, that you are so merry upon, this hair, and this figure, have so much virtue in them, that I live perfectly quiet, do as I will, and keep what company I like. The ignorant and illiterate are disgusted with my appearance. The foppish and effeminate never come near me. My chief companions are men of good manners, modesty, and virtue; for it is such that I love. I never knock at the gates of the great; I laugh at their coronets, their purple, their pride, and themselves. How can you think of ridiculing this habit, which is not only the ornament of good men, but even of the very gods? Look at their images, and tell me which of us they most resemble, you or me. If you examine, you will find, that, not only in the Grecian temples, but also amongst Barbarians, the gods are represented with hair and beards as I am, and not shaved like you. You will observe also, that many of them have no more coat than I have. How then could you think of debasing the habit, which becomes the gods?

⁎ It

⁎ It is easier to know how than when to write or transcribe a note. "Hard words," as Dr. Johnson teaches, " are only hard to those who understand them not;" and books, we know, are made of words. But let not the learned be angry. What is useless to them may not be impertinent to others. There was once a time, when their taste was less fastidious. Amongst readers of inferior attainments, if there should chance to be one with just the same share of understanding and knowledge, neither more nor less than what served to produce this translation and these notes, he may here have the pleasure of being flattered with the contemplation of kindred ideas. He will see, that the book might have been much better, and will be able to point out the effects sometimes of inattention, sometimes of inability. Yet his sympathy will not persecute, because his judgment cannot praise.

NOS HÆC NOVIMUS ESSE NIHIL.

THE END.

www.ingramcontent.com/pod-product-compliance
Lightning Source LLC
Chambersburg PA
CBHW020334240426
43673CB00039B/933